Module 12

Using Assessment to Guide Instruction (Grade 3–Adult)

Louisa C. Moats, Ed.D.

BOSTON, MA • NEW YORK, NY • LONGMONT, CO

09 08 07 06 05 1 2 3 4 5

ISBN 1-59318-200-7

Printed in the United States of America

Published and Distributed by

SOPRIS WEST

EDUCATIONAL SERVICES

A Cambium Learning™ Company

4093 Specialty Place • Longmont, Colorado 80504
(303) 651-2829 • www.sopriswest.com

191MOD12

Dedication

To Steve, without whom my work would be impossible,
and with whom I have joy in every day.

—LCM

Acknowledgments

LETRS has been developed with the help of many people. At Sopris West, I continue to enjoy the first-class capabilities of Toni Backstrom, LETRS Program Director, and the expertise of editorial and publishing staff, including Lynne Stair, Karen Butler, Tyra Segars, and many others. Michelle LaBorde has contributed extraordinary talent to the design and development of the LETRS CDs. The vision and commitment of Stuart Horsfall, Ray Beck, Chet Foraker, Stevan Kukic, and Steve Mitchell enabled LETRS to have been created.

The National LETRS trainers have helped me improve LETRS and deliver the professional development with fidelity. I am most grateful to Carol Tolman, Susan Hall, Anne Cunningham, Marcia Davidson, Marsha Berger, Deb Glaser, Judi Dodson, Anne Whitney, Nancy Hennessy, Mary Dahlgren, Joan Sedita, Linda Farrell, and Susan Smartt for their wisdom, hard work, and companionship in the LETRS endeavor.

Pati Montgomery and the teachers and students of Eiber Elementary School in Colorado collaborated with Sopris West Educational Services in the filming of support videos and the contribution of case study material. They also showed us that the ideas represented in the modules can be applied to the benefit of all students.

Finally, I am grateful to all my colleagues across the country who campaign for the improvement of teacher preparation and professional development.

—LCM

About the Author

Louisa C. Moats, Ed.D., is a nationally recognized authority on how children learn to read and why people fail to learn to read. Widely acclaimed as a researcher, speaker, consultant, and teacher, Dr. Moats has developed the landmark professional development program LETRS for teachers and reading specialists.

Between 1997 and 2001, she completed four years as site director for the National Institute of Child Health and Human Development's Early Interventions Project in Washington, D.C., under the direction of Barbara Foorman of the University of Texas. The project included daily work with teachers and students in high-risk, low-performing schools. Dr. Moats spent the previous 15 years as a licensed psychologist and certified school psychologist in private practice in Vermont, evaluating people of all ages and walks of life for academic learning problems.

Dr. Moats began her professional career as a neuropsychology technician before becoming a teacher. She earned her master's degree at Peabody College of Vanderbilt and a doctorate in reading and human development from the Harvard Graduate School of Education. She has been a faculty member at St. Michael's College in Vermont and Simmons College in Boston, and Clinical Associate Professor of Pediatrics at the University of Texas, Houston.

In addition to LETRS, Modules 1–12 (Sopris West Educational Services, 2005, 2006), her authored and coauthored books include:

- *Spelling: Development, Disability, and Instruction* (York Press, 1995)
- *Straight Talk About Reading* (with Susan Hall; Contemporary Books, 1998)
- *Speech to Print: Language Essentials for Teachers* (Brookes Publishing, 2000)
- *Parenting a Struggling Reader* (with Susan Hall; Random House, 2002)

Instructional materials include the Scholastic Spelling program and *Spellography* (Sopris West Educational Services, 2002). Dr. Moats has written numerous journal articles and policy papers, including the American Federation of Teachers' "Teaching Reading *Is* Rocket Science." She continues to focus on the improvement of professional development for teachers through her work with LETRS.

Dr. Moats and her husband divide their time between Idaho and Vermont. Their extended family includes a professional skier, a school psychologist, an alpaca rancher, and an Australian shepherd.

Contents for Module 12

Overview of LETRS: Language Essentials for Teachers of Reading and Spelling

Our national goal of "every child a reader" requires teachers with expertise in reading instruction. The research-based, comprehensive instructional programs called for by Congress are necessary tools to reach the goal, but no program is sufficient without continuous, long-term professional development for teachers. Teaching reading is a complex discipline that requires content and procedural knowledge beyond the use of a program manual.

To reach all learners, teachers must understand: (a) how students learn to read and write; (b) the reasons why some students fail to learn; and (c) the instructional strategies best supported by research. Teachers also need to understand the language structures they are teaching. The American Federation of Teachers' "Teaching Reading *Is* Rocket Science" (Moats, 1999) and the Learning First Alliance's "Every Child Reading: A Professional Development Guide" (2000) endorsed these core understandings. LETRS modules are designed to teach teachers the content outlined in such consensus documents on reading instruction. These instruments use professional development methods successful with diverse groups of teachers: regular classroom and special education, novice and expert, rural and urban.

The 12 stand-alone modules of LETRS address each component of reading instruction—phoneme awareness; phonics, decoding, spelling, and word study; oral language development; vocabulary; reading fluency; comprehension; and writing—and the foundational concepts that link these components. The characteristics and needs of English language learners (ELLs), dialect speakers, and students with other learning differences are addressed throughout the modules. The format of instruction allows for deep learning and reflection beyond the brief "once-over" treatment these topics are typically given.

Experienced staff developers can teach each module in one day, although follow-up reading, study, review, and classroom application is strongly recommended. A number of commercially available reading curricula provide appropriate classroom and tutorial methods for teaching structured language. The LETRS program is not intended to replace these basal and supplemental programs, but to help teachers implement them well, fill gaps in their instructional programs, and adapt instruction for the full range of learners in any class.

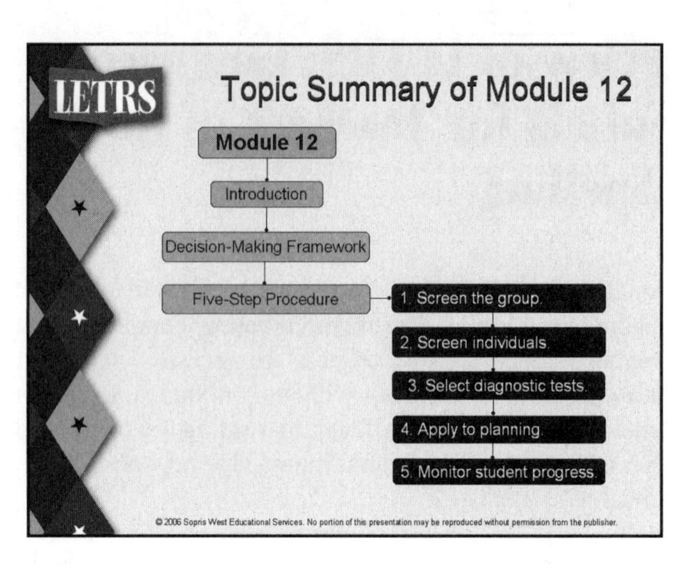

Slide 3

Topic Summary

LETRS Module 12 reviews the rationale and procedures of brief language, reading, spelling, and writing assessments that will inform classroom and remedial instruction. Teachers must use precious time well; thus, this module—grounded in current research—emphasizes the importance of efficient, reliable, and valid assessments about reading problems that will help pinpoint the needs of at-risk students. Specific steps to accomplish this goal—classroom screening; individual screening; and individually administered diagnostic tests that measure phoneme and morpheme awareness, decoding and word analysis, spelling, written composition, reading fluency, and comprehension—are demonstrated and rehearsed.

Although assessment should drive instruction, one cannot use assessments purposefully without a strong background in: (a) how students learn to read; (b) what causes reading problems; and (c) what is included in the content of instruction. LETRS Modules 1–11 are designed to provide that background.

LETRS

Goals for Module 12

- Become familiar with appropriate assessment tools.
- Plan to screen students efficiently.
- Group students for instruction.
- Select appropriate programs, methods, and materials.
- Plan to monitor progress and adapt instruction.

Slide 4

After taking this module, participants should be more knowledgeable about:

- Assembling a group of suitable assessments for classroom and individual use.
- Following a strategic plan for screening students and finding those who need intervention.
- Grouping students for instruction and deciding on the resources needed to help individuals.
- Selecting appropriate instructional programs, methods, and materials for those students.
- Planning and monitoring the progress of students on skills and reading fluency.

"We have lots of information technology. We just don't have any information."

Table 12.1. The Content of LETRS Modules Within the Language-Literacy Connection

Components of Comprehensive Reading Instruction ↓	Organization of Language						
	Phonology	Morphology	Orthography	Semantics	Syntax	Discourse and Pragmatics	Etymology
Phonological Awareness	2	2					
Phonics, Spelling, and Word Study	3, 7	3, 7, 10	3, 7, 10				3, 10
Fluency	5		5	5	5		
Vocabulary	4	4	4	4	4		4
Text Comprehension		6		6	6	6, 11	
Written Expression			9, 11	9, 11	9, 11	9, 11	
Assessment	8, 12	8, 12	8, 12	8, 12	8, 12	8, 12	

LETRS

Take the Module 12 Pretest

- We will return to the Pretest at the end of the day.

Slide 5

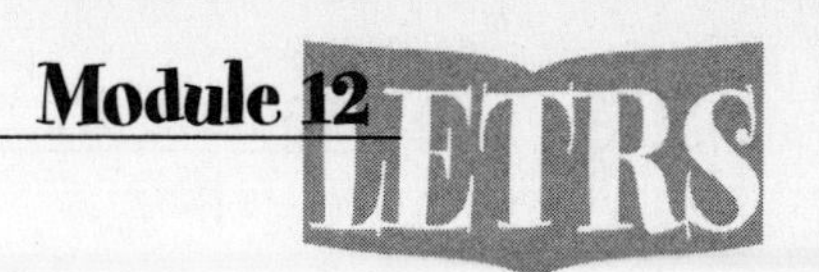

Module 12 Preview (Pretest!) Questions

1. What is the purpose of a screening assessment?

2. If you are screening a new class of students, what assessments do you typically use?

   a. Do you know if their reliability and validity are established?

   b. Are you concerned about the reliability, validity, efficiency, or relevance of your screening program?

   c. Do you consider the time spent in screening to be reasonable in relation to the value of the information you gain about each student?

3. Have you and your team established what constitutes a "benchmark" standard—the minimal "grade level" reading achievement—that you expect students to attain?

4. If you find out that a student's passage reading comprehension is below grade level, what other questions do you then ask about the student's problems and instructional needs?

____

____

____

5. Why would you (or would you not) give a direct measure of phonological skills—especially phoneme identity, segmentation, and blending—to a student in grade 3 and beyond?

____

____

____

6. Do you feel well informed about your students' challenges with reading comprehension?

____

____

____

7. Based on the assessment data you now collect, in what ways do you typically alter your instructional plans for students?

____

____

____

Introduction: What Should We Assess?

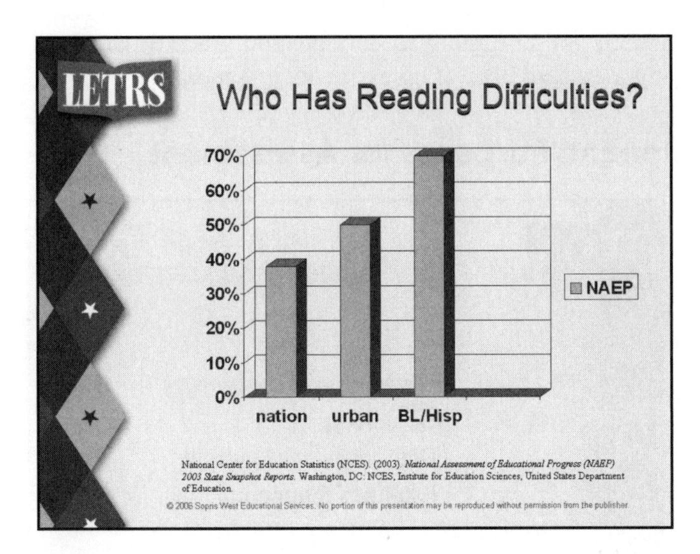

Slide 6

Reading Problems Are Common but Treatable

Reading problems affect about 4 out of 10 students nationally in the intermediate grades and beyond. In some schools and districts, the rate of reading failure is as high as 70% (National Center for Education Statistics, 2003). The reading challenges of many students prevent them from benefiting from education and affect them for life. Thus, if anything is to be done about the poor reading skills of many students—especially ELLs; students of poverty; Black, Hispanic, and American Indian students; and students who attend low-performing schools—instruction must be as focused, intensive, and research-based as possible. And research *does* show that significant improvement is possible in students who have poor reading skills; in most cases, the pattern of failure is treatable (Moats, 2001; Torgesen, Rashotte, Alexander, Alexander, & MacPhee, 2003; Torgesen, 2004).

"Instruction" here refers to whole-group and small-group work of the regular classroom teacher, as well as to the supportive efforts of support personnel and specialists including reading teachers, special education teachers, speech-language therapists, volunteers, and paraprofessionals. Instruction based on student needs can be planned and delivered effectively if appropriate assessments have been conducted (Fuchs & Fuchs, 2003). Of the many possible tools available to assess student reading, a few should be selected for specific purposes validated by current reading research. Otherwise, the time and energy of both teachers and students can be squandered in endless testing that ultimately leads to no significant improvement in overall reading achievement.

The assessment process and methods presented here are designed to help teams of administrators and regular and special educators to: (a) screen classrooms efficiently; (b) select students who may need more intensive instruction in reading and related skills; and (c) plan instructional interventions. However, before we can discuss the procedures, tools, and uses of assessments for struggling readers beyond grade 3, we should review the varying aims and uses of assessments in general.

Types of and Purposes for Assessment

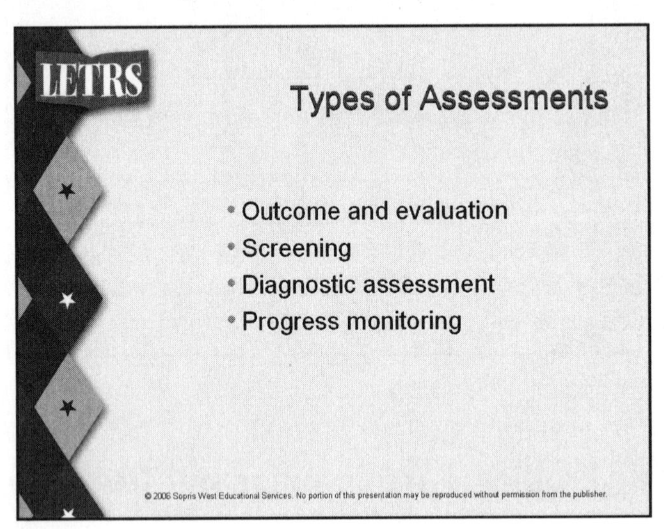

Slide 7

"Do you swear to tell the truth, the whole truth, and nothing but the truth, and not in some sneaky relativistic way?"

Outcome Assessments

Outcome, or summative, assessments are "high-stakes," end-of-year accountability tests, now required of states who are complying with the provisions of the No Child Left Behind legislation. These assessments usually measure reading achievement with silent passage reading and multiple-choice comprehension questions. The assessments are given to groups and are usually administered under time constraints. Assessment results are reported as standard scores, percentiles, and normal curve equivalents so that consumers can tell where an individual student stands in relation to normative data for his or her age group. New state initiatives and those funded with Reading Excellence, Title 1, School Improvement, and Reading First funds require districts to demonstrate improvement with students "at risk" and to meet adequate yearly progress (AYP) goals. End-of-year tests—such as the Stanford 9, Iowa Test of Basic Skills, Terra Nova, and Metropolitan Achievement Tests—are often used for this purpose.

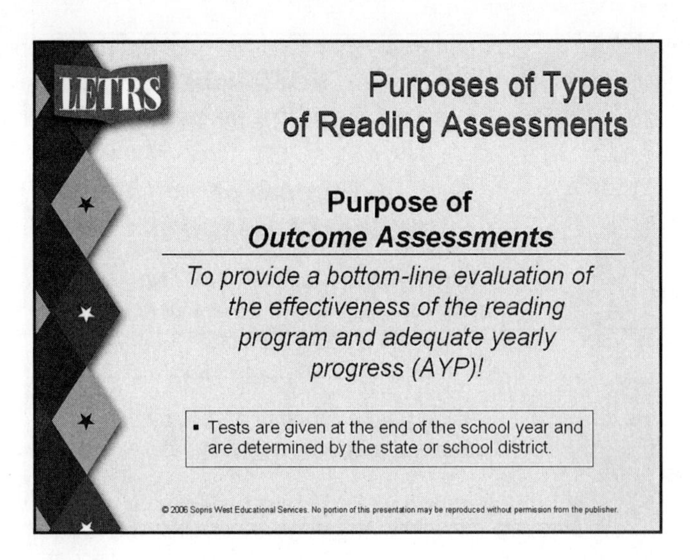

Slide 8

Outcome tests given by districts and states reflect the end result of curriculum design, program implementation, and individual teachers' efforts over the course of an entire school year. If such assessments are delayed until the end of third or fourth grade, planning and implementing interventions for poor readers is a more costly and less effective enterprise than early intervention in kindergarten (Torgesen et al., 2003). Schools can and should know how many students are likely to meet state standards far in advance of the spring date on which the yearly outcome tests are given, and programs to help students at risk should have been in place throughout the year.

Outcome tests for older students almost always involve silent reading of a passage of several paragraphs and multiple-choice comprehension questions that follow. Few outcome measures for older students include tests of the underlying skills necessary to become a proficient reader, such as word recognition accuracy and fluency or alphabetic knowledge. In the standards movement of the late 1990s, many states rewrote their literacy standards to enumerate component skills that must be mastered by students learning to read; however, those standards assume that intermediate and older students have mastered the skills enumerated for the lower grades, such as letter recognition, phonological awareness, and reading fluency. Thus, if a student scores below grade level on the high-stakes annual summative test, it is not possible to determine the causes for the reading difficulty. Low passage comprehension scores may be a manifestation of poorly developed basic reading skills, and a teacher cannot know where a student's problem lies without directly assessing critical components of proficient reading to see where the breakdown occurred.

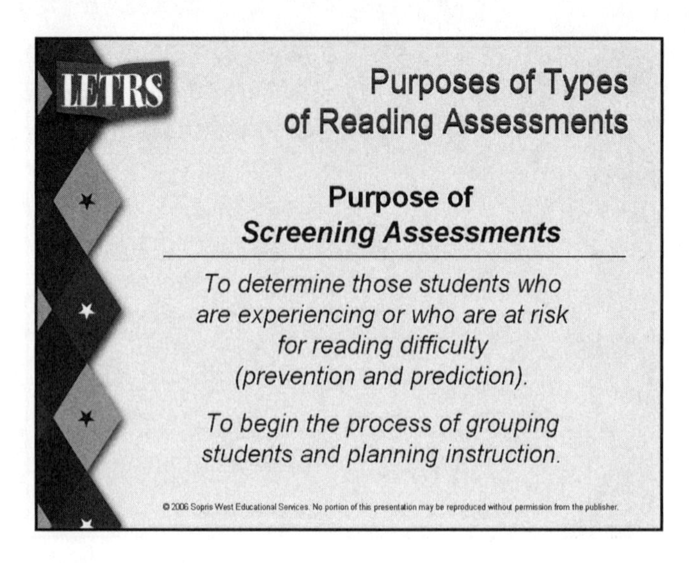

Slide 9

Screening Assessments

Screening assessments are designed to identify student abilities efficiently and effectively *before students fail* or *before they establish a pattern of failure* in the younger grades (Torgesen, 2004). Screenings can also be used to: (a) identify older, poor readers; (b) estimate the degree of a student's reading difficulty; and (c) determine what other assessments might be necessary to understand a student's instructional needs. A valid screening measure, or group of measures, will be a good *predictor* of performance on high-stakes, summative tests, and will help teachers determine the intensity, type, and duration of outcomes-oriented intervention.

Both component reading skills and passage reading comprehension can be measured in screening assessments. An important assumption underlying the validity of any screening is that silent reading comprehension is accounted for or can be predicted on the basis of component reading skills. Component reading skills such as speed and accuracy of word recognition can be measured much more briefly and efficiently than silent reading comprehension and can give us a reliable indicator of who needs additional assessment.

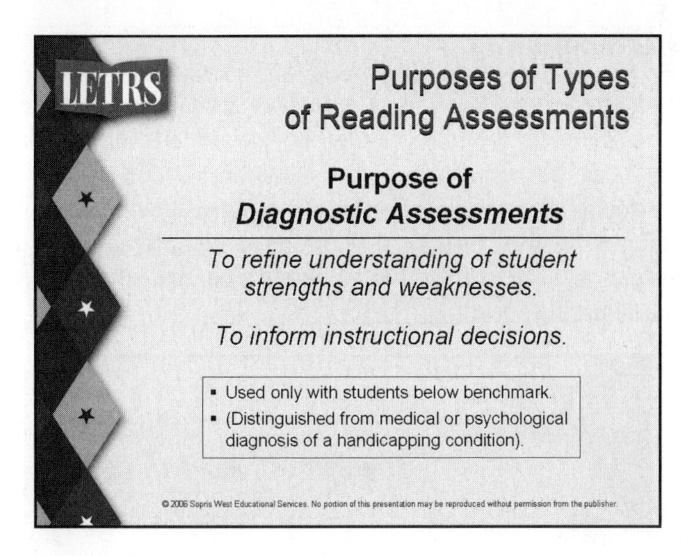

Slide 10

Diagnostic Assessments

The term *diagnostic assessment* has two meanings: First, it refers to the use of informal surveys and standardized tests that sample a student's in-depth academic knowledge and skill so that teachers can group like students together and focus their instructional planning. Second, it refers to the activity of classifying a handicapping condition or disorder according to diagnostic criteria established by a profession such as psychiatry, psychology, or speech-language pathology. We will use the term *diagnostic assessment* to mean assessment, through both formal and informal means, of a student's instructional needs.

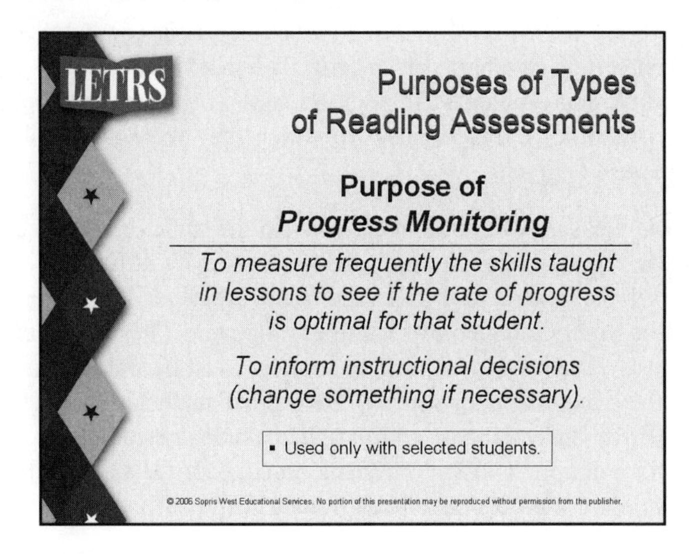

Slide 11

Progress Monitoring

Progress monitoring assessments are given frequently to students who have been screened, found to be well below grade-level, and have been assigned to an intervention program. In order to determine whether a given instructional program is working to bring a student closer to a target or benchmark level of reading skill, progress can monitored as much as once a week or once every other week with equivalent forms of a task, such as oral passage reading fluency.

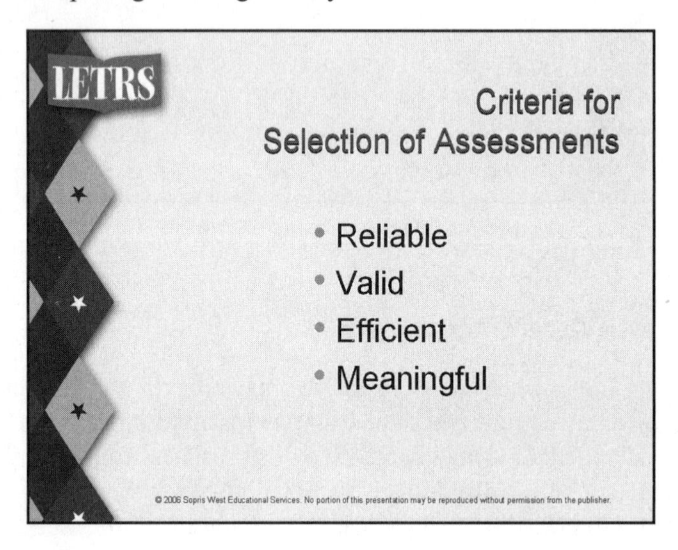

Slide 12

Criteria for Selecting Assessments

In order to be most useful in a school setting, assessments of any kind must meet certain psychometric criteria. The most important are **reliability**, **validity**, and **efficiency**. In addition, assessments must be **meaningful** in order to serve the *purpose* for which they were designed and for which the test is given.

A **reliable** measure would be likely to yield the same result if it could be given twice on the same day in the same context by different examiners. In other words, reliable tests give results that are dependable—results that will not be highly affected by examiner judgment. Thus, when examiner judgment is called for in scoring, examiners must be trained sufficiently so that their judgments or scoring are similar to those of other trained people. Error analysis (i.e., attributing a student error to a particular cause), for example, is often unreliable in educational and psychological testing unless examiners have been trained sufficiently to agree with one another.

A **valid** measure corresponds well to other known, valid measures (concurrent validity) and predicts with good accuracy how students are likely to perform on an accountability measure (predictive validity). A valid assessment also measures what it purports to measure. For example, if the assessment claims to be one of oral reading fluency and no calculation of reading speed or accuracy is included, the measure is probably not valid for the purpose of estimating reading fluency. If a measure cannot be shown to correspond with other accepted measures of reading outcomes, it probably is not a valid indicator of overall reading ability.

An **efficient** measure can be given at a relatively low cost in relatively little time. If a teacher is asked to spend an hour assessing each student in the class, the procedure is, by definition, inefficient. It takes too long, especially in relation to the usefulness of the information that can be gained.

"I understood each and every word you said but not the order in which they appeared."

Finally, measures are **meaningful** when used for a specific purpose. Many hours can be wasted gathering assessment data that are irrelevant to instruction. The purposes of the assessment strategies and practices advocated in this module are to: (1) inform instructional choices; (2) assist with grouping of students with like abilities in the classroom; and (3) determine if students are responding to instruction. The response to intervention (RTI) approach to allocation of remedial and special education dollars is dependent on judicious use of such measures.

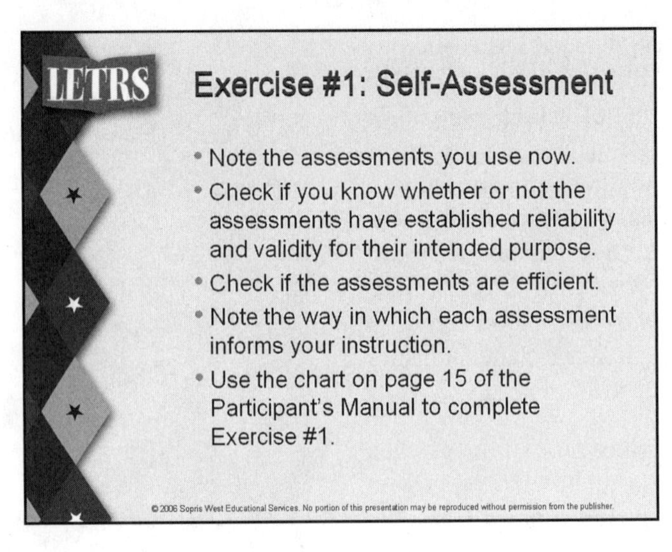
LETRS
Exercise #1: Self-Assessment
Note the assessments you use now.
Check if you know whether or not the assessments have established reliability and validity for their intended purpose.
Check if the assessments are efficient.
Note the way in which each assessment informs your instruction.
Use the chart on page 15 of the Participant's Manual to complete Exercise #1.
© 2006 Sopris West Educational Services. No portion of this presentation may be reproduced without permission from the publisher.

Slide 13

Exercise #1: Self-Assessment

- Note and describe what assessments you use now.
- In a small group, briefly compare your assessment approach to that of others.

Name of Measure	Valid and Reliable?	Efficient?	Useful for What Purpose?

A Framework for Assessing Struggling Readers of Any Age

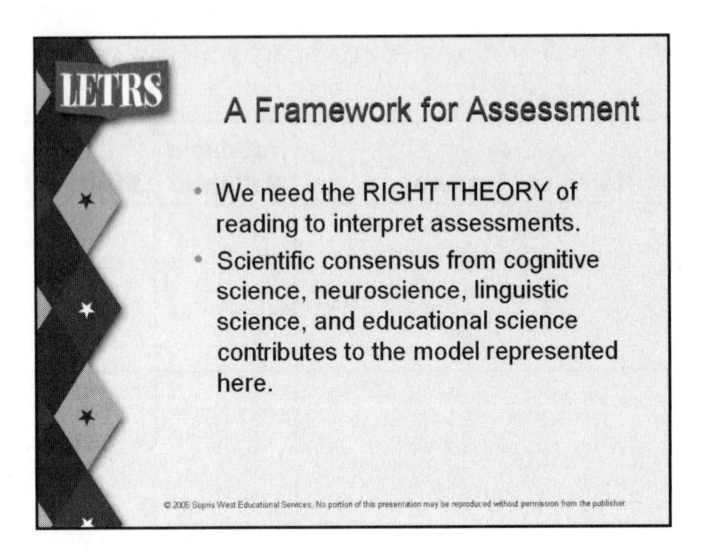

Slide 14

Cognitive-Linguistic Processes Necessary for Reading

With national attention focused on the prevention and treatment of reading problems in the primary grades, teachers and education leaders often question whether the research pertaining to early reading has any relevance for understanding older, poor readers. "What do we do with all those students in grade 4 and up who cannot read?" ask those who are responsible for them. Although research on older, poor readers is less voluminous than research on beginning reading, tenets emanating from scientific reading research also pertain to understanding older students.

Reading difficulties experienced by students beyond third grade, whether minor or serious, can be understood within models of reading processes grounded in interdisciplinary, longitudinal, replicated, scientific studies. One widely respected model of those reading processes—the outcome of 20 years of cognitive psychological research—is depicted below. This model was the basis for Marilyn Adams' award-winning[1] book, *Beginning to Read: Thinking and Learning About Print* (Adams, 1990). Recently it was featured again in an issue of *Psychological Science in the Public Interest* that was devoted to an overview of the ways in which cognitive science informs reading instruction (Rayner, Foorman, Perfetti, Pesetsky, & Seidenberg, 2001). Information about the brain processors is discussed and illustrated in Shaywitz's (2003) book.

1 "Outstanding Contribution to Educational Research" award from the American Educational Research Association.

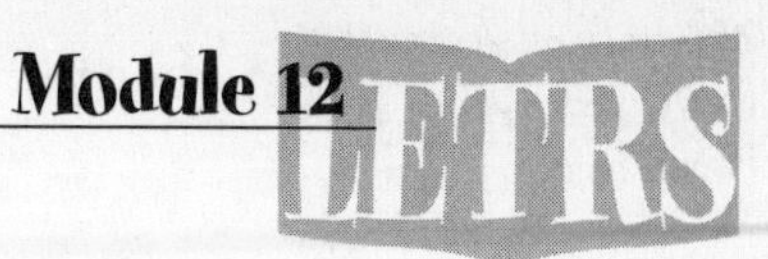

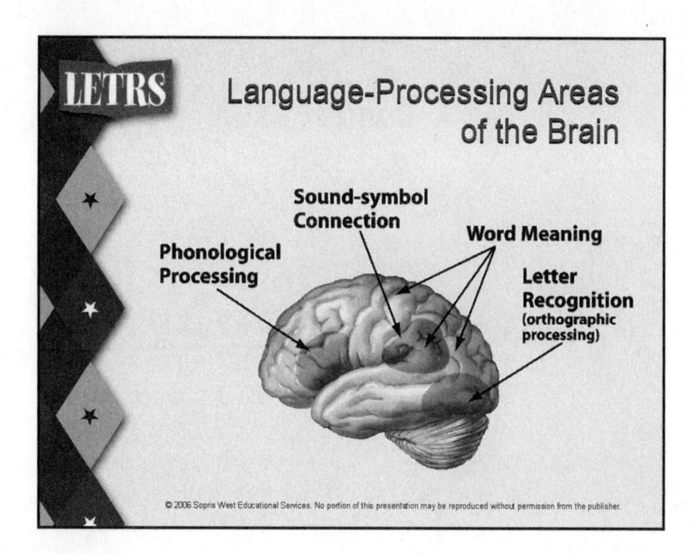

Slide 15

Reading is an acquired language skill; that is, a large proportion of our students need systematic help in learning how to read. Reading problems may originate in any one of, or all four, essential language-processing systems, as the diagram below suggests.

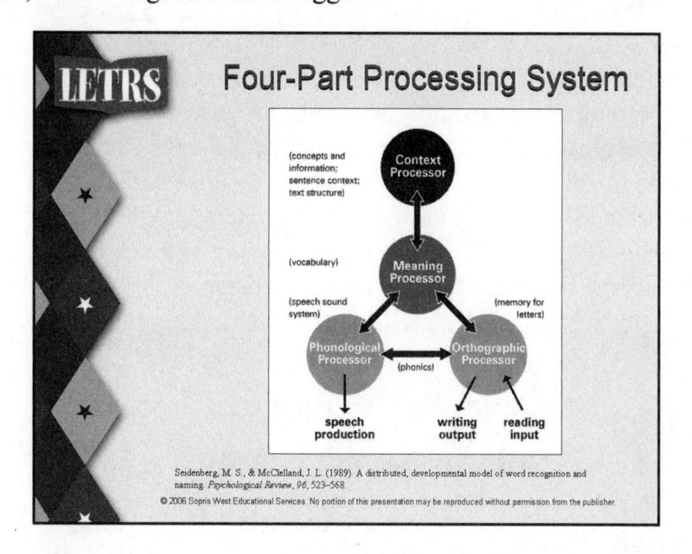

Slide 16

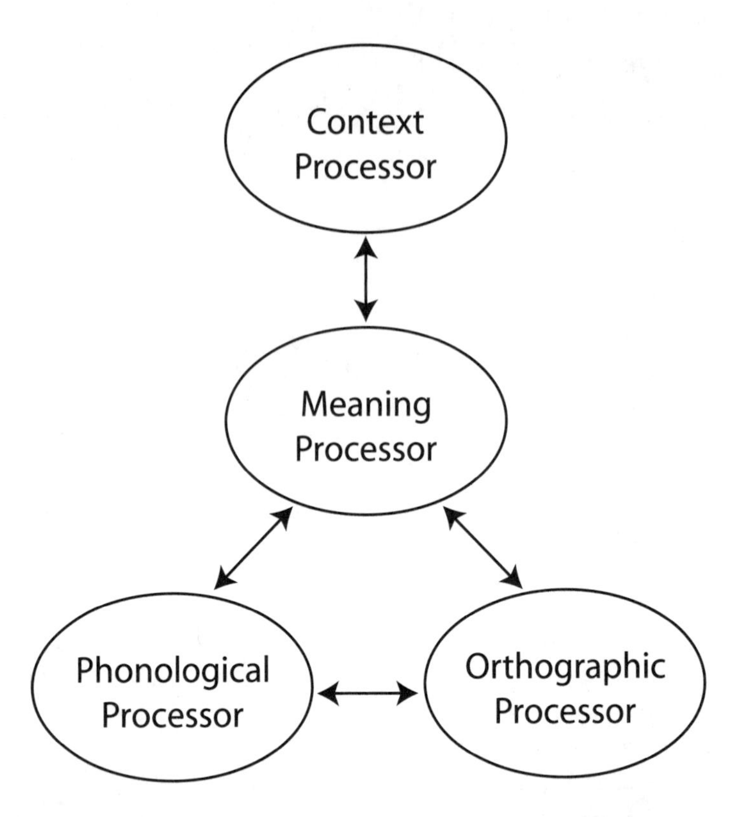

Phonological processing weaknesses are characteristic of the large majority of poor readers—especially those with more serious reading disabilities. Phonological processing is important because it is the underpinning for "cracking the code," or learning how to recognize printed words. Underdeveloped skills in the other three systems contribute to reading problems as well, and ultimately, all processing systems must be proficient to support fluent reading for comprehension.

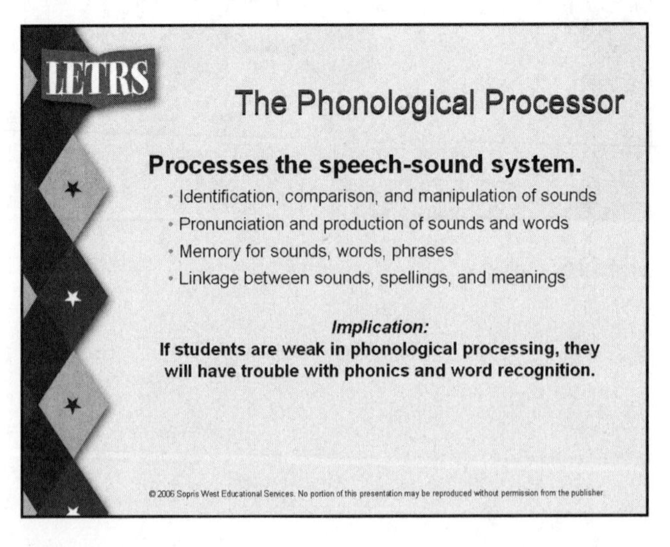

Slide 17

The Phonological Processor

This neural network, located primarily in the left frontal lobe of the brain, enables us to perceive, remember, interpret, and produce the speech-sound system of our own language and learn the sounds of other languages as well. The phonological processor allows us to imitate and produce stress patterns, including the rise and fall of the voice during phrasing. It is responsible for such functions as:

- Remembering the words in a phrase or the sounds in a word.
- Comparing words that sound similar, such as **medicate** and **meditate**.
- Retrieving specific words from our mental dictionaries (lexicon) and producing the speech sounds in those words.
- Holding the sounds of a word in memory so that a word can be written down.
- Taking apart the sounds in a word so that they can be matched with alphabetic symbols.

The phonological processor detects, stores, and retrieves the phonemes and sound sequences in spoken language. The ability to learn phonics and to match printed words with spoken language is highly dependent on adequate phonological processing in the beginning stages of reading. Sounds must be linked to print, however, and the orthographic processor must be activated if graphemes or letter sequences are to be detected, stored, and recalled for reading and writing.

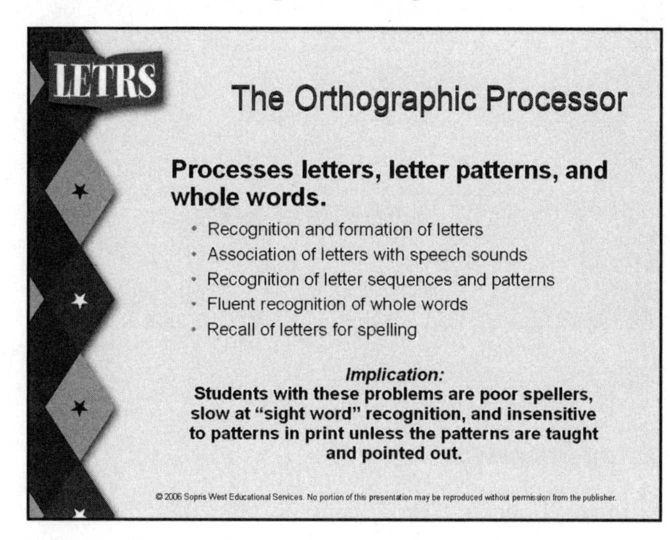

Slide 18

The Orthographic Processor

The orthographic processing system, located primarily in the occipital, or back, part of the cerebral hemispheres of the brain, visually perceives and recognizes letters, punctuation marks, spaces, letter patterns, and words. We rely on the orthographic processor when we copy lines of print, recognize meaningful parts of words, or process words as whole units. Spelling depends on orthographic memory. When we look at print, its features are filtered, identified, and matched to images of letters or letter sequences already in memory. If the letters or letter sequences are familiar, we associate them with sounds and meanings. We have no trouble interpreting widely varying print forms, including individual handwriting styles, type fonts, or uppercase and lowercase letters. The size, style, and case of print are not major factors in word recognition once a reader knows letters and letter-sound relationships.

The orthographic processing system stores information about print that is necessary for word recognition and spelling. The speed with which letters are recognized and recalled is very important for proficient reading. In functional neuroimaging (fMRI) studies, the back part of the brain in proficient readers is activated as printed words are recognized. Obviously, however, print images must be associated with word meanings for fluent reading to occur.

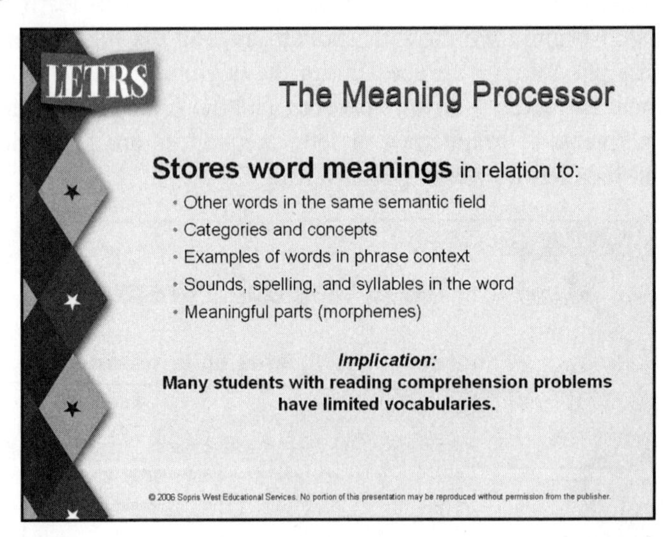

Slide 19

The Meaning Processor

According to the Four-Part Processing System model of printed word recognition, the phonological processor, orthographic processor, and meaning processor must communicate with one another rapidly and accurately for fluent reading to occur. We can connect sounds to print without meaning (e.g., when we "read" a foreign language without knowing what the words mean, read nonsense words, or read a new word by sounding it out), but unless the meaning processor is accessed, no comprehension is

possible. The meaning processor stores and retrieves the words we know and also constructs the meanings of any new words that are named during reading. The context of the passage and other information supports the construction of those meanings.

A word filed in the mental dictionary is multidimensional; its image has sound, spelling, morphological structure, and syntactic role. The meaning processor is structured according to a number of semantic organization features, such as synonym relationships, roots and other morphemes, spelling patterns, common meaning associations, and connotations. It expands and reorganizes itself as new vocabulary is learned.

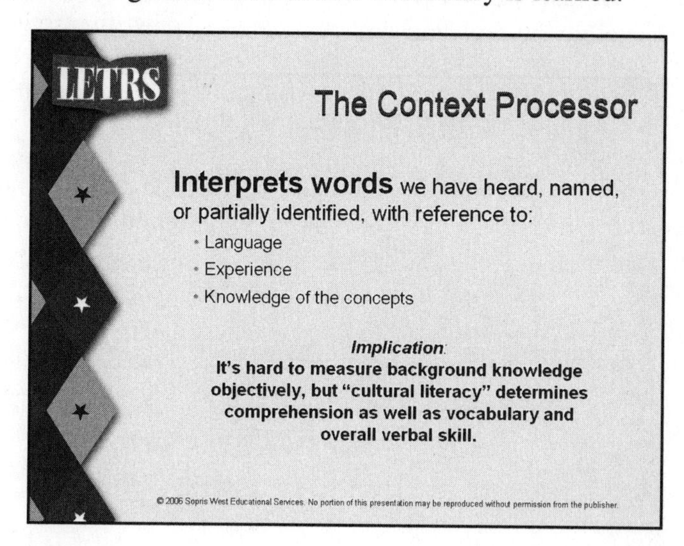

Slide 20

The Context Processor

The context processor influences the construction of meaning during reading. Words are embedded in phrase, sentence, and discourse contexts. They also are used within knowledge domains that are represented in our minds as mental images, propositional structures, and other associations to life experience. The context provides the referent for a word's meaning. For example, many words have multiple meanings, but only one is used within a specific sentence. The spelling of a word such as **passed** or **past** is determined by its meaning in the context of a sentence: *The quarterback passed the ball to the tight end for the touchdown.* Context helps us to rapidly find a meaning in our mental dictionary once a word has been named: *That idea provided a* segue *between the introduction and the body of the speech.* Context has only a very limited role in facilitating word-naming itself. Word recognition and pronunciation are primarily the job of the phonological and orthographic processors.

Using a Cognitive-Linguistic, Developmental Model of Reading to Guide Assessment

Again, reading is a language function; reading and writing differ from oral language because the brain must decode written alphabet symbols to access meaning. Reading problems originate in most students because one or more prerequisite language skills was never sufficiently developed. Assessment that is guided by knowledge of the language proficiencies needed to support reading development—and the order in which the proficiencies are typically acquired—can pinpoint students' instructional needs and save valuable time. Overall language proficiency in students is strongly related to their reading skill.

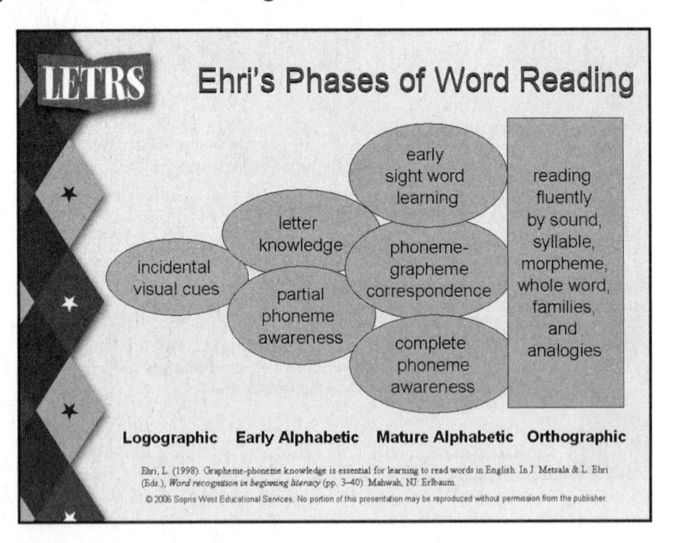

Slide 21

Phonological awareness is prerequisite for identifying the separate speech sounds in words. Identifying the separate speech sounds is necessary for understanding what letters in an alphabet represent. Recognition of common letter combinations and patterns that are used to represent sound combinations is necessary for reading larger "chunks" of words. Recognition of larger chunks—syllable patterns and meaningful word parts or morphemes—is necessary for fast word recognition. Recognition of many words by sight is necessary for text reading fluency. Fluency, in turn, allows attention to be devoted to comprehension. Vocabulary is a vital part of comprehension, because without individual word meanings, the language of text cannot be understood. Thus, the whole cognitive structure of reading is learned in a more or less predictable progression.

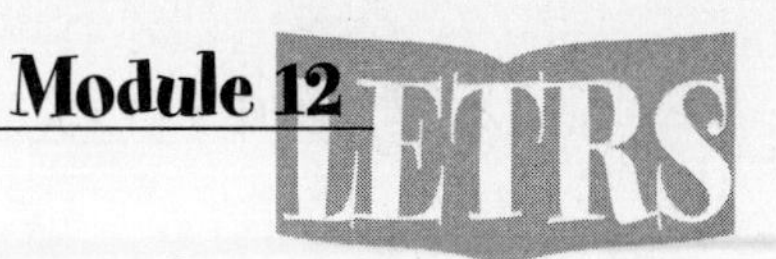

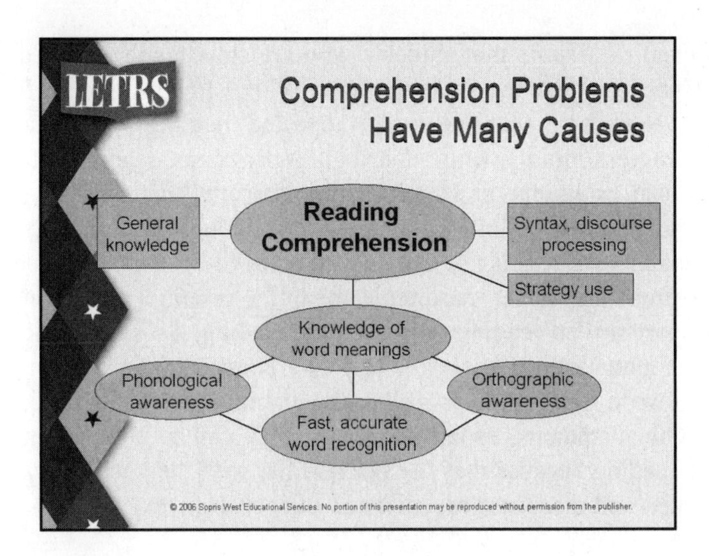

Slide 22

Comprehension of connected text is predicted by adequate reading fluency. If a student's reading fluency is less than the minimal rate necessary to support comprehension, then the cause of that dysfluency must be determined before targeted instruction is possible. Using the Four-Part Processing System as a guide, we can infer that any student's lack of reading comprehension and/or fluency might have one or more causes:

1. Insufficient general knowledge or insufficient knowledge of the topic of discussion (experiential context).
2. Insufficient knowledge of the forms of academic language in which the message is expressed (linguistic context).
3. Insufficient knowledge of the meanings of individual words in a passage (vocabulary or word meaning).
4. Insufficient capacity to recognize printed words accurately and automatically (orthographic processing).
   i. Underdeveloped knowledge of phoneme-grapheme links.
   ii. Slow naming speed.
   iii. Underdeveloped knowledge of letter patterns, syllable patterns, and morphemes in print.
5. Insufficient capacity to remember printed words because of underdeveloped phonological awareness or phonological memory (phonological processing).
6. Insufficient practice with reading, with no underlying skill weaknesses or knowledge or language deficiencies.

It is logical to assume that students who are slow readers for reason #6 simply need to practice reading more. With straightforward fluency-building exercises, such as timed repeated readings,[2] such students should progress rapidly. Book-distribution programs, reading incentives, motivational programs, and multimedia programs that provide practice at the student's instructional level should be enough to promote success. Unfortunately, success is not that easy to achieve for many dysfluent students because they never mastered some of the essential underlying skills that support skilled reading. Higher-level reading skills are undermined by poor foundations in speech-sound awareness, phonic decoding skill, and sight word recognition as well as the inability to decode multisyllabic words. Other students, especially ELLs, may fail to comprehend what they are reading because they are not familiar with the vocabulary, phrasing, syntax, and discourse organization of academic text.

All of these variables can be assessed—some directly, some indirectly—so that valuable instructional time can be used to each student's greatest advantage. If a student's comprehension is low and fluency is below benchmark, then we must determine which of the six reasons stated above is most likely to be the cause of the student's difficulty. Through direct and efficient assessment, we can determine whether instructional time is best spent: (a) rebuilding foundation skills in word recognition; (b) focusing on vocabulary and language comprehension; (c) getting up to speed in passage reading; or (d) an integrated combination of those activities.

Assessment of foundational word recognition skills, a prerequisite for fluent reading, can explore which of the following building blocks might be weak and need to be reconstructed:

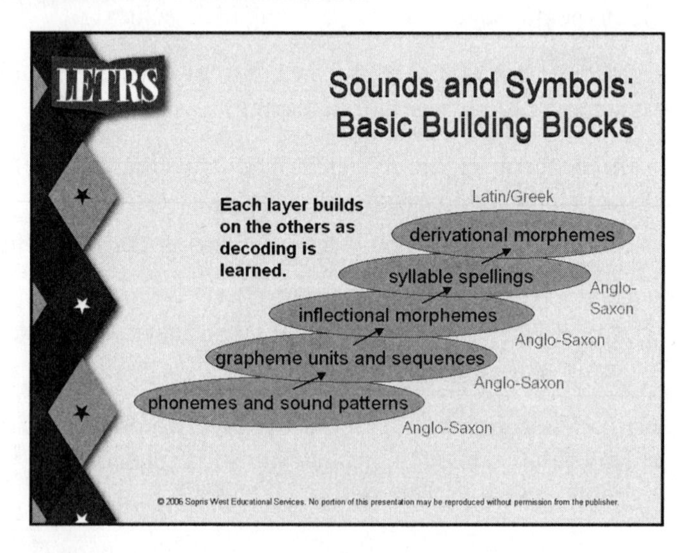

Slide 23

[2] See LETRS Module 5—Getting Up to Speed: Developing Fluency—for a detailed treatment of instructional techniques.

Table 12.2. Steps in Teaching and Learning Printed Word Recognition in English

<table>
<tr><td></td><td></td><td></td><td></td><td></td><td></td><td colspan="2">Greek-Derived Morphemes</td></tr>
<tr><td></td><td></td><td></td><td colspan="4">Derivational Morphology: Anglo-Saxon and Latin Roots, Prefixes, Suffixes</td><td></td></tr>
<tr><td></td><td></td><td colspan="2">Inflectional Morphology</td><td></td><td></td><td></td><td></td></tr>
<tr><td></td><td></td><td colspan="2">Common Syllables Syllabication</td><td></td><td></td><td></td><td></td></tr>
<tr><td></td><td colspan="2">Fluent Recognition of Word Families</td><td></td><td></td><td></td><td></td><td></td></tr>
<tr><td></td><td colspan="2">300–500 Sight Words</td><td></td><td></td><td></td><td></td><td></td></tr>
<tr><td colspan="3">Phoneme-Grapheme Correspondences</td><td></td><td></td><td></td><td></td><td></td></tr>
<tr><td colspan="3">Phonological Awareness</td><td></td><td></td><td></td><td></td><td></td></tr>
<tr><td>K</td><td>1</td><td>2</td><td>3</td><td>4</td><td>5</td><td>6</td><td>7+</td></tr>
</table>

LETRS

Exercise #2: Grouping Students You Know

- Do your current assessment practices allow you to pinpoint with reasonable accuracy the components of reading and writing that students are having the most trouble with?
- Try placing your students on the graph on page 26, relying just on your memory.

Refer to the next slide for a copy of this graph.

Slide 24

Exercise #2: Grouping Students You Know

- Think of a group of students you are currently teaching, have taught in the past, or consult with now.
- Write the first name or initials of each student in the box that most closely approximates the level of ability in each literacy category. (A student can be placed in more than one box.)
- How do you validate where these students place?

	Spelling and Production of Written Language	**PA, Phonics, and Decoding Skill**	**Fluency**	**Vocabulary and Reading Comprehension**
Strong, established				
Mild weaknesses				
Serious weaknesses				

A Progressive Strategy for Assessing Reading Components

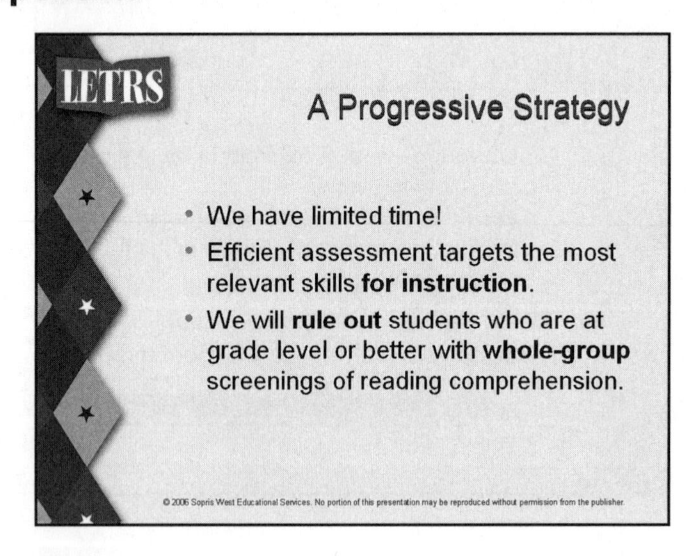

Slide 25

If we had unlimited time with each student to explore every aspect of a reading problem, we would seek to gather information about all of the relevant domains that could contribute to the student's difficulties (see Table 12.3 below). To do so would require many hours, however, and it would be—and is—very expensive. Thorough, individual diagnostic work-ups would also compete for the limited time available to teach students what they need to learn. All school personnel with the requisite qualifications would be spending the bulk of their time doing student assessments instead of directing their energy, time, and resources to instruction. Therefore, a strategy for screening students would help educators avoid unnecessary assessment.

The progressive decision-making strategy delineated in the remainder of this module is possible because of what is known about reading development. Briefly put, fluent reading with good comprehension depends on the integrated use of multiple subcomponent skills: letter, letter pattern, word, phrase, sentence, and passage level (Wolf et al., 2003). At the letter, letter pattern, and word levels, phonological, orthographic, and morphological processes must be intact; at the phrase, sentence, and passage levels, semantic and syntactic processing must be intact. Thus, the assessment approach starts from the desired goal (reading grade-level passages for meaning), to the most closely correlated skill (oral passage reading fluency), to the underlying factors that could cause problems and that might need remediation.

Table 12.3. Domains for a Diagnostic Reading Assessment Conducted for the Purpose of Categorizing a Disability and Determining Educational Programming[3]

Domain for Assessment	Information to Be Gathered
Family and Individual History	◆ Other family members who had difficulty learning to speak, read, write, and spell ◆ Health or medical impairments to learning ◆ Any delays in developing spoken language in preschool ◆ Parents' concern about speech, language, motor skills, or attention span ◆ Other languages spoken at home and level of English language proficiency in the home
Cognitive Ability, or Intellectual Aptitude (IQ)(now considered optional; not necessary for a diagnosis of reading disability)	◆ Either a Wechsler (WISC-III, WAIS-III) or Stanford-Binet IQ test; possibly the Woodcock-Johnson® Tests of Cognitive Abilities ◆ Test should measure individual's aptitude for learning in verbal, logical, mathematical, visual-motor, visual-spatial, symbolic, memory, and attentional domains

[3] This table is based on one that first appeared in Hall and Moats, *Parenting a Struggling Reader*, Random House (2000).

Domain for Assessment	Information to Be Gathered
Oral Language Proficiency, including Phoneme Awareness	◆ Speech sound and syllable awareness ◆ Word pronunciation ◆ Word retrieval ◆ Rapid naming of letters, numbers, colors, objects ◆ Knowledge of word meanings ◆ Comprehension and production of sentence structure (syntax) ◆ Expressive verbal ability, including organization of ideas, elaboration, and clarity of expression ◆ Comprehension of what is heard and read
Reading Comprehension	◆ Timed readings of longer passages read silently ◆ Ability to summarize, answer multiple-choice questions, or complete cloze tasks (fill-in-the-blanks in a passage)
Single-Word Decoding (phonic knowledge) and Reading Fluency	◆ Ability to read single words out of context under timed and untimed conditions ◆ Application of phonic and morphologic word attack to reading non-sense words (timed and untimed) ◆ Oral paragraph-reading fluency and accuracy
Spelling	◆ Dictated spelling test (not multiple choice) ◆ Developmental spelling inventory ◆ Analysis of errors for speech-sound omission, letter-sequence confusion, and poor memory for common words
Written Composition	◆ Composition of a story or an essay for students capable of writing more than a few sentences ◆ Analysis of word choice, conceptual organization, sentence quality, elaboration of ideas, grammar, and use of punctuation and capitalization ◆ Informal tasks, such as writing a paraphrase, combining simple sentences into compound and complex sentences, writing an outline and summary of a passage, or writing part of a structured paragraph
Handwriting	◆ Ability to form letters, both individually and in words ◆ Fluency of alphabet production ◆ Consistency and slant of letters ◆ Right- or left-handedness

Procedure for Conducting Reading Assessments

LETRS

Five-Step Procedure

1. Screen the whole class.
2. Screen individual students, and use the data to sort students into two main groups.
3. Select and administer diagnostic (educational) tests for students who need them.
4. Group students and plan instruction.
5. Use progress monitoring.

Slide 26

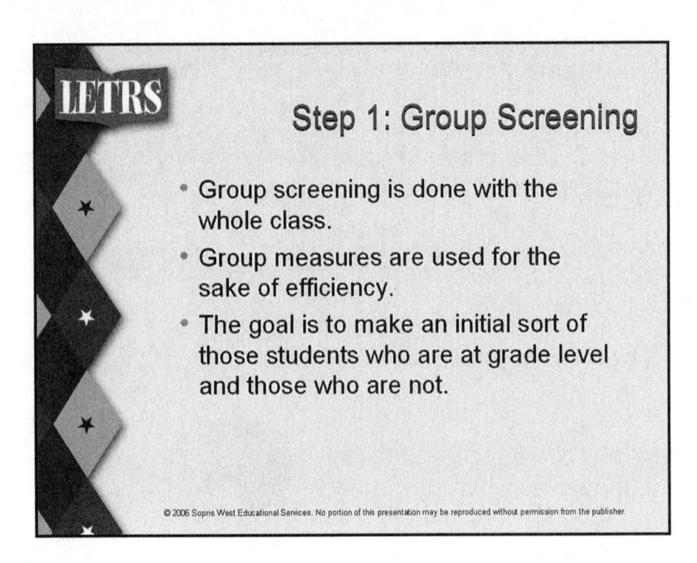

Slide 27

Step 1: Group Screening

Where does one start? It is not necessary to test all of the domains listed in Table 12.3 unless one is conducting a lengthy assessment for special education services or other medical or psychological treatment. The first goal of assessment is to decide who needs more intensive small-group or individual instruction; then, appropriate student groupings can be formed.

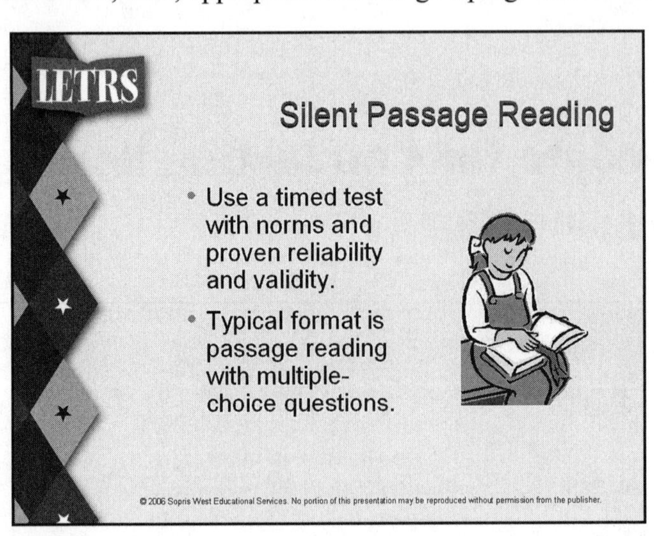

Slide 28

Silent Passage Reading Comprehension

A time-limited, silent passage reading test can be given to whole classes and is a good screening tool. Silent passage reading tests usually accompany core, comprehensive reading programs, but many of those have no standardization data to allow comparisons with a national normative

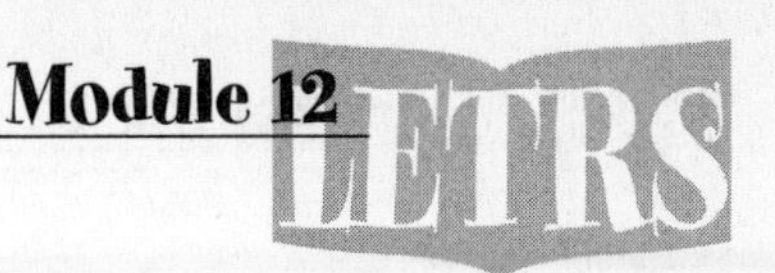

sample. Silent passage reading tests that do allow comparisons to national norms and that meet acceptable standards of technical adequacy include:

- Gates-McGinitie Reading Tests®
- Iowa Test of Basic Skills
- Stanford Achievement Test (9th ed.)
- *TerraNova* CAT™
- Nelson-Denny Reading Test (for high school students and adults only).

Publisher-supplied placement tests can also be used in the beginning of the year, although the quality and accuracy of those tests (concurrent validity) vary widely. Unit tests given every six–eight weeks may also be used to flag students who are not progressing as expected, but those results should be supplemented and verified with other measures given individually. Students who score below the 40th percentile should be flagged as possible candidates for supplemental reading, language, and/or writing instruction.

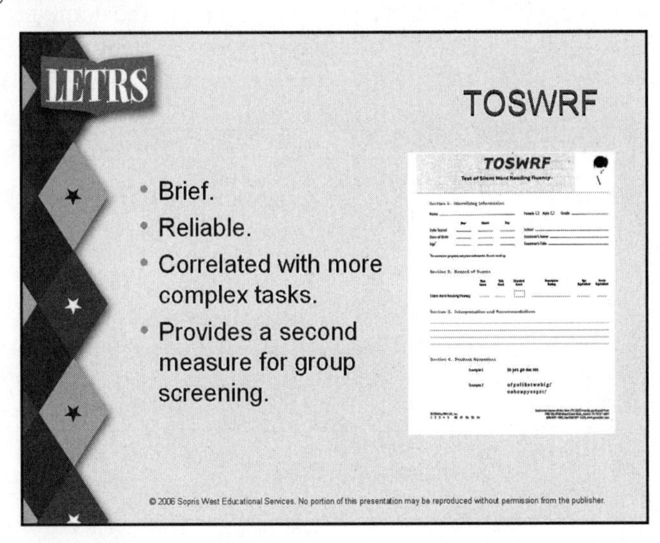

Slide 29

Test of Silent Word Reading Fluency (TOSWRF)

A new measure of word recognition proficiency that can be given to student groups as a silent reading test is the TOSWRF (Mather, Hammill, Allen, & Roberts, 2004). It consists of a simple task that is highly correlated with more complex reading tests. Students are given three minutes to draw lines between the boundaries of printed words that are run together; the words are ordered by progressive reading difficulty. (Forms are available for both pretesting and posttesting.) The test is easy to administer and score, and the results give a strong indication of overall reading proficiency.

LETRS

Exercise #3: Experience the TOSWRF

- Try the TOSWRF.
- You'll be given two minutes (actual test is three minutes).
- Draw a line between adjacent words.

Review the directions on the next slide before you begin.

Slide 30

Exercise #3: Experience the TOSWRF

- Below is an excerpt from the Test of Silent Word Reading Fluency.

- When the presenter says "Go," draw a vertical line between as many of the words as you can. You will be given two minutes to try this sample. (Please note that users of the test must follow standardized administration and scoring procedures and use the forms provided by the test makers.)

TOSWRF

Test of Silent Word Reading Fluency

Section 1. Identifying Information

Name ______________ Female ☐ Male ☐ Grade ______________

	Year	Month	Day
Date Tested	____	____	____
Date of Birth	____	____	____
Age*	____	____	____

School ______________

Examiner's Name ______________

Examiner's Title ______________

*For normative purposes, use years and months. Do not round up.

Section 2. Record of Scores

	Raw Score	%ile Rank	Standard Score	Descriptive Rating	Age Equivalent	Grade Equivalent
Silent Word Reading Fluency	____	____	☐	____	____	____

Section 3. Interpretation and Recommendations

____

____

____

____

Section 4. Student Responses

Example 1 in yes go me see

Example 2 ofgoliketwobig/
onheupyesget/

1 2 3 4 5 08 07 06 05 04

Additional copies of this form (#11262) may be purchased from PRO-ED, 8700 Shoal Creek Blvd., Austin, TX 78757-6897 800/897-3202, Fax 800/397-7633, www.proedinc.com

Exercise #3: Experience the TOSWRF (continued)

Sample Exerpt

leakjudgehoundtightbuiltcoachfresh/

breezebulbawfulmountelvesbirthwake/

swungmoundrentguestgullbulgenurse/

saucequiltnavymurmurzerogravykettle/

tigercouncilfolktuckplumjunglerhythm/

limblilyrovemothlungfueldazzlemercy/

symbolboltclenchbluffhullgermthrive/

neglectnudgefleshlurchvarietylaurel/

drenchpulsegriefyachtquizstaffcycle/

emberbulkquarrycounseljurypeltfilm/

strictdepthmuzzlefudgefícklefilter/

lureutterbluntvaryreekgaugeutilize/

jeernymphgiltpoachwieldprivacyfrenzy/

molarlynchracialaccessgildjauntsurly/

ebbdivulgegaietystaunchcliqueevolve/

envoydirgedelvebaublenaiveductvigil/

girthfoiblefeignauravoguetautdefer/

fetterlewdlenientcysthulkdetervie/

wreakcommunaldurespreceptelixir/

sullyseculargirddubcoerceguile/

epochprecludepulsarvernacularquaff/

symposiumrazeimbuejunctureneophyte/

encomiumfecundacquiescejocund/

egressimbrogliocajolepecuniaryfacile/

Slide 31

Spelling Achievement (Group Administered)

In general, spelling and reading skills are correlated with one another, although some students are much better readers than they are spellers. Spelling is also a strong predictor of reading skill. A standardized spelling measure can be given to groups of students to obtain scores that allow comparisons of students to their national peer group. The Test of Written Spelling-4, the Wide Range Achievement Test (Spelling), and the Kaufman Test of Educational Achievement can all be used for this purpose. Each of these tests requires the teacher to dictate a list of words, ordered by difficulty. The percentile ranks and standard scores obtained are based simply on the number of words spelled correctly.

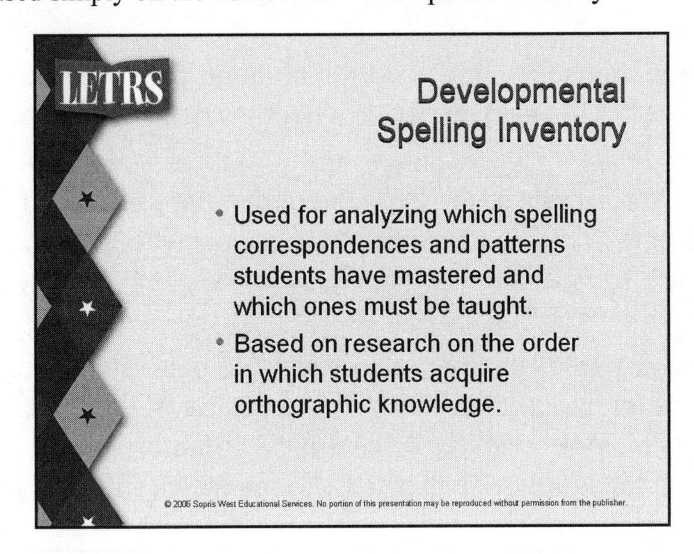

Slide 32

Developmental Spelling Inventory

Developmental spelling inventories do not yield standard scores and percentile ranks but rather are used to determine which phoneme-grapheme correspondences and which orthographic patterns the student has learned and needs to learn. The results indicate that the developmental spelling level and skills to emphasize in instruction are: (a) speech sound awareness; (b) sound-symbol correspondences; (c) high-frequency words; (d) spelling patterns; (e) ending rules; and/or (f) morphology. In addition to the inventory included in this module, *Words Their Way* (Bear, Invernizzi, Templeton, & Johnston, 2003) includes several kinds of spelling inventories that are well validated for directing word study (word analysis and spelling) instruction.

The following inventory is used in the *Spellography* program (Moats & Rosow, 2002):

Directions for Administering a Spelling Inventory

This inventory is not a placement test and not a test of memorized words. Instead, it is designed to reflect what students in grades 3–7 understand about the building blocks of accurate spelling.

Administration. Do not teach the words directly before giving this inventory. Give only as many words as your students can attempt to write with reasonable success. You can give the first 15 words on one day, score the results, and give the next set of words to students who get at least 10 of those right.

Say the word, use it in a sentence, and then repeat the word. Ask students to say the word out loud themselves. Tell students this test is to help you decide what they need to learn next.

Scoring. To use the individual score sheet, circle each listed feature that the student writes correctly. Count only features that are noted on the score sheet. Each correct feature is worth one point. Add an extra point in the next-to-right-hand column for words spelled correctly.

Interpretation. Given every few months, this inventory can reflect small gains in response to instruction that are not always visible on standardized tests. If students "have" a feature, such as digraphs, that will be obvious when you look down the score sheet. The features, listed left to right, are in approximate developmental order, so it will be easy to see where students are secure and where instruction needs to begin. Start by reviewing the features and correspondences the student knows, then design lessons to emphasize the level at which the student is breaking down.

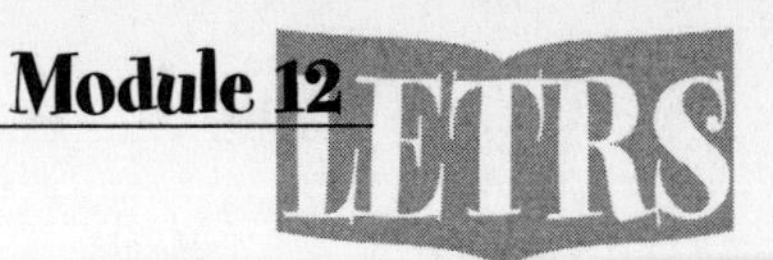

2/16/2003

Spellography Set B
Tutorial B Period Name Ben

1. thift
2. still
3. trunk
4. clock
5. string
6. skicth
7. choke
8. grade
9. slite
10. qwake
11. sneak
12. couch
13. birnt
14. splice
15. barge
16. cwout
17. slugh
18. moest
19. swerol
20. yoahnjg
21. drag
22. tracing
23. showerd
24. quiting
25. ixpest
26. suden
27. bunneys
28. trakshen
29. enstructer
30. atendence
31. cranfeshen
32. reportabal
33. detents
34. fexe bal

Spelling Inventory // Set B – Individual Score Sheet

Name: ______________________ Date________

FEATURES	Short vowel	Digrph Trigrph	Blend	VCE	Complex Cons.	Vowel + R	Vowel Teams	Inflec-tions	Syllable juncture	Prefix	Final Syllable / suffix	Root morph	Extra Point/ correct	Point Totals
1. theft	e	th	ft											
2. still	i		st		ll									
3. trunk	u		tr/nk											
4. clock	o	-ck	cl											
5. string	i	-ng	str											
6. sketch	e	-tch	sk											
7. choke		ch		o-e										
8. grade			gr	a-e										
9. slight			sl				igh							
10. quake			qu	a-e										
11. sneak			sn				ea							
12. coach		-ch					oa							
13. burnt			nt			ur								
14. splice			spl	i-e										
15. barge					-ge	ar								
16. quote			qu	o-e										
17. sludge	u		sl		-dge									
18. moist			-st				oi							
19. swirl			sw			ir								
20. yawning							aw	ing						
21. dragged			dr					-ed	gg					
22. tracing			tr					-ing	a-(e)					
23. showered		sh				er	ow	-ed						
24. quitting								-ing	tt					
25. expressed								-ed		ex		press		
26. sudden									dd		-en			
27. bunnies								-ies	nn					
28. traction											-tion	trac		
29. instructor										in	-or	struct		
30. attendance										at	-ance	tend		
31. confession										con	-sion	fes(s)		
32. reportable						or				re	-able	port		
33. difference										dif	-ence	fer		
34. flexible											-ible	flex		
#/Color Code	/7	/7	/19	/5	/3	/5	/6	/7	/5	/6	/8	/8	/34	/120

Feature totals in bottom row are colored in as follows: Red= 2+ errors; Yellow = 1 error; Green = 0 errors

2

LETRS

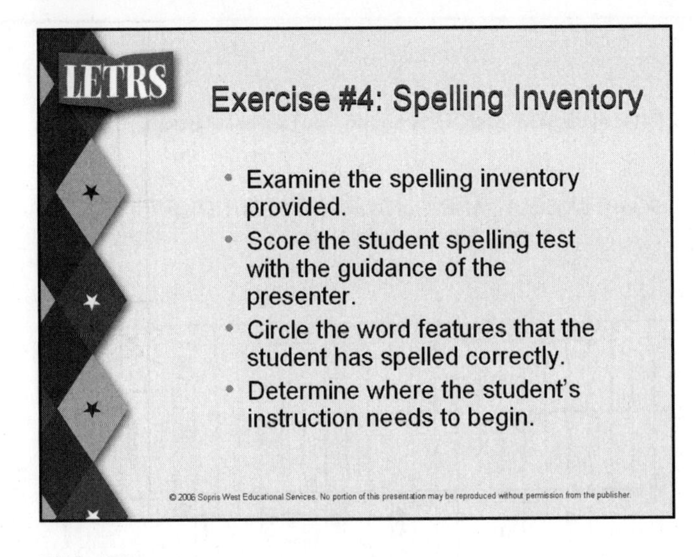
LETRS
Exercise #4: Spelling Inventory
• Examine the spelling inventory provided.
• Score the student spelling test with the guidance of the presenter.
• Circle the word features that the student has spelled correctly.
• Determine where the student's instruction needs to begin.
© 2006 Sopris West Educational Services. No portion of this presentation may be reproduced without permission from the publisher.

Slide 33

Exercise #4: Spelling Inventory

- Score the spelling inventory and summarize the student's instructional needs.
- When you're finished, compare your score sheet to the completed score sheet in Appendix A.

Spelling Inventory // Set B – Individual Score Sheet Name: ________________ Date______

FEATURES	Short vowel	Digrph Trigrph	Blend	VCE	Complex Cons.	Vowel + R	Vowel Teams	Inflec-tions	Syllable juncture	Prefix	Final Syllable / suffix	Root morph	Extra Point/ correct	Point Totals
1. theft	e	th	ft											
2. still	i		st		ll									
3. trunk	u		tr/nk											
4. clock	o	-ck	cl											
5. string	i	-ng	str											
6. sketch	e	-tch	sk											
7. choke		ch		o-e										
8. grade			gr	a-e										
9. slight			sl				igh							
10. quake			qu	a-e										
11. sneak			sn				ea							
12. coach		-ch					oa							
13. burnt			nt			ur								
14. splice			spl	i-e										
15. barge					-ge	ar								
16. quote			qu	o-e										
17. sludge	u		sl		-dge									
18. moist			-st				oi							
19. swirl			sw			ir								
20. yawning							aw	ing						
21. dragged			dr					-ed	gg					
22. tracing			tr					-ing	a-(e)					
23. showered		sh				er	ow	-ed						
24. quitting								-ing	tt					
25. expressed								-ed		ex		press		
26. sudden									dd		-en			
27. bunnies								-ies	nn					
28. traction											-tion	trac		
29. instructor										in	-or	struct		
30. attendance										at	-ance	tend		
31. confession										con	-sion	fes(s)		
32. reportable						or				re	-able	port		
33. difference										dif	-ence	fer		
34. flexible											-ible	flex		
#/Color Code	/7	/7	/19	/5	/3	/5	/6	/7	/5	/6	/8	/8	/34	/120

Feature totals in bottom row are colored in as follows: Red= 2+ errors; Yellow = 1 error; Green = 0 errors

2

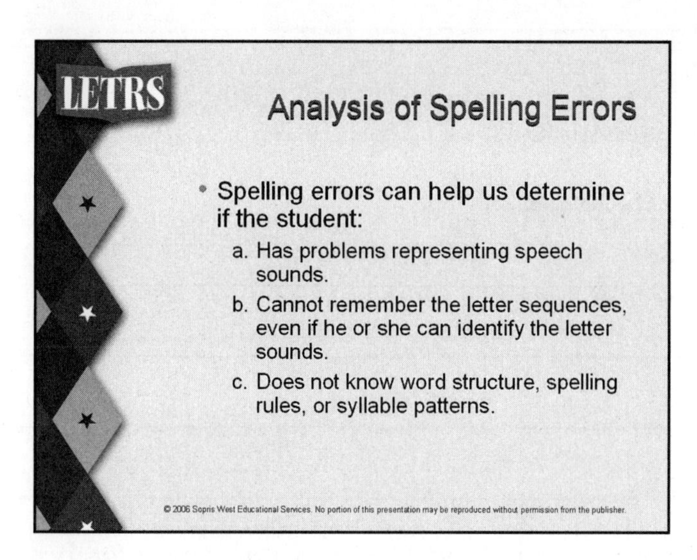

Slide 34

Analysis of Spelling Errors

Students' spelling errors are rich sources of information about their language processing and their instructional needs (Masterson & Apel, 2000). Students who have weak phonological skills will substitute, omit, and/or change the order of sounds in words. Students who are phonologically aware but still have trouble remembering letters and letter sequences will spell phonetically (each sound represented), using the wrong letters or letter patterns. Students whose linguistic awareness problems are at a higher level of word structure, syllabication, and morphology, may not recognize or produce the stable spellings of meaningful parts of words—compounds, base words and endings, and prefixes, suffixes, and roots in Latin and Greek-based words.

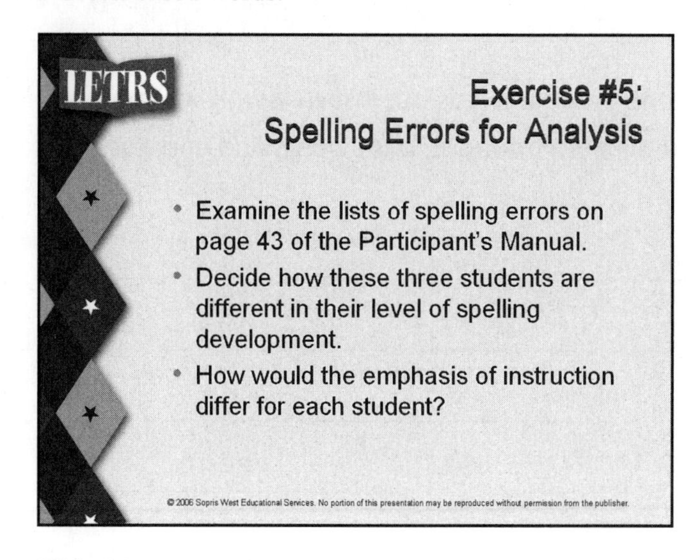

Slide 35

Exercise #5: Spelling Errors for Analysis

- Below are spelling errors typical of three students.

1. Which student is phonologically challenged?

2. Which student is generally aware of the sounds but uses the wrong letters for those sounds and does not know rules for adding endings?

3. Which student is quite solid on one-syllable words but insecure with written syllable patterns, endings, and word structure (compounds, base words and endings, prefixes, suffixes, roots)?

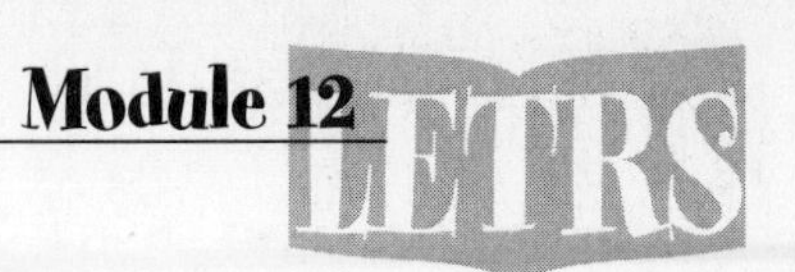

Words Given	Student #1	Student #2	Student #3
speck	spek	sbek	speck
switch	swich	sich	switch
throat	throte	trot	throat
nurse	nurs	nrs	nurse
scrape	skrape	sap	scrape
charge	chardge	jarj	charge
phone	fone	fon	phone
smudge	smuge	suj	smuge
point	poit	pt	point
squirt	skwirt	st	squirt
drawing	droughing	gwiig	drawwing
trapped	chrapt		trapted
waving	waiveing		waveing
powerful	pourfull		powerfull
battle	badl		battel
fever	fevr		feaver
lesson	lesin		
pennies	penees		
fraction	frakshun		
sailor	saler		

LETRS

Structured Writing Sample

- Students are given the same prompt.
- Some scaffolding is provided (e.g., brief brainstorm or discussion, provision of a title).
- Students are given a time limit to write the best composition they can.
- Scoring is done according to a rubric or set of descriptive criteria and examples.

Slide 36

Structured Writing Sample

A structured writing sample is one in which students are given a topic, along with a few minutes of preparation for writing, and a time limit to do the best job they can with that topic. If composing a structured writing sample is required of the whole class on a regular basis, the samples can be scored to measure progress in written composition according to an accepted rubric. The well-known 6+1 Trait™ Writing model of the Northwest Regional Educational Laboratory (www.nwrel.org/assessment/pdfRubrics/6plus1traits.pdf) for example, includes a rubric for judging the quality of student writing on these dimensions: ideas, organization, voice, word choice, sentence fluency, conventions, and presentation. Some states have adopted their own rubrics for judging writing samples. Beyond a qualitative rubric that scores these dimensions of writing, a student's command of language can be informally judged.

Depending on their instructional history, students should also be given a minute to write the entire alphabet in manuscript and/or cursive. This is an easy way to determine if students possess the most basic writing skills, letter formation skills, and knowledge of the alphabet.

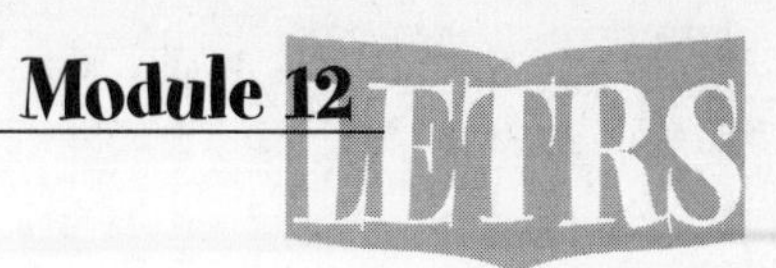

Table 12.4. Framework for Judging a Structured Writing Sample

Stages of the Writing Process	6+1 Trait™ Writing Model (Northwest Regional Educational Laboratory)	Component Language, Cognitive and Motor Skills
Planning/Organization	Ideas	♦ Knowledge of background information ♦ Memory for information
	Organization	♦ Knowledge of genre form and conventions (e.g., narrative/expository) ♦ Logical reasoning and use of logical connectors ♦ Goal orientation and topic focus
Drafting/ Transcription	Word Choice	♦ Size and depth of vocabulary ♦ Retrieval and naming ability ♦ Use of specific content words ♦ Use of figurative language
	Voice	♦ Awareness of audience's needs (perspective-taking) ♦ Self-knowledge ♦ Ability to speak with conviction and persuasiveness ♦ Pragmatic language ability
	Sentence Fluency	♦ Formulation of: complete, varied sentences; compound and complex sentences ♦ Grammatical conventions ♦ Conventional punctuation and capitalization symbols ♦ Letter-formation and handwriting fluency ♦ Verbal working memory to support on-line production and monitoring of output
Revision/ Editing	Conventions	♦ Phonological awareness for phonetic spelling accuracy and self-monitoring of transcription ♦ Memory for high-frequency word spellings and spelling patterns ♦ Knowledge of conventions of grammar and usage ♦ Skill at using resources
	Presentation	♦ Spatial organization ♦ Design ♦ Communicative intent ♦ Audience awareness

LETRS

Student Writing Sample

Name T.L. Grade 5 (CASE STUDY #2) Date

- Write a story about the first birthday you can remember. Describe what your day was like and how it felt to be one year older.

My Birthday Was gud becuse I had all my frends at my pote. my frend chris and my frend mick. we eat cack and ice crem. we plad futboll. We rod bics

We will examine writing samples in case studies toward the end of this module.

Slide 37

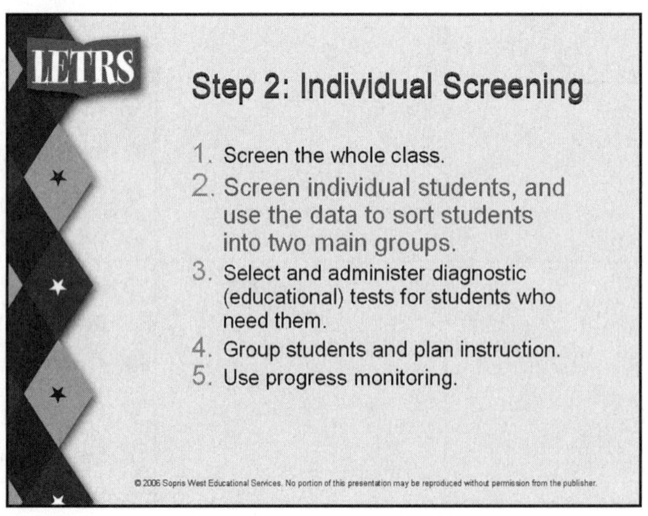

Slide 38

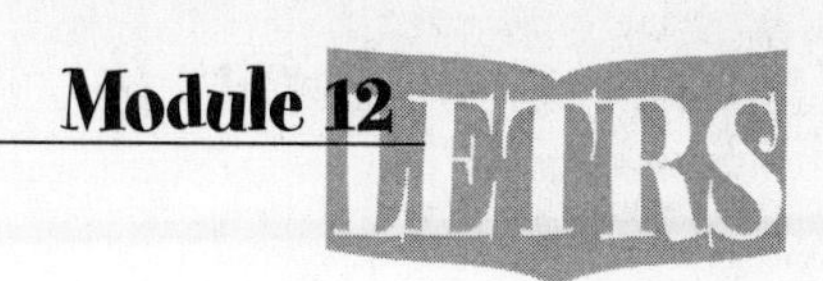

Step 2: Individual Screening

Timed Oral Passage Reading

If students score below average (below the 40th percentile) on group-administered screenings, then further assessment should be undertaken. The next most efficient, direct, and valid step is to give a timed oral reading measure to each student who appears to be at risk (Deno, Fuchs, Marston, & Shin, 2001; Good & Kaminski, 2002; Hosp & Hosp, 2003). One-minute oral reading fluency measures are highly correlated with more complex and lengthy reading comprehension tests (Fuchs & Fuchs, 2003). Words correct per minute (WCPM) on an oral reading test is a simple statistic that predicts performance on high-stakes, end-of-year outcome tests of reading comprehension. Screening assessment is not complete without this measure.

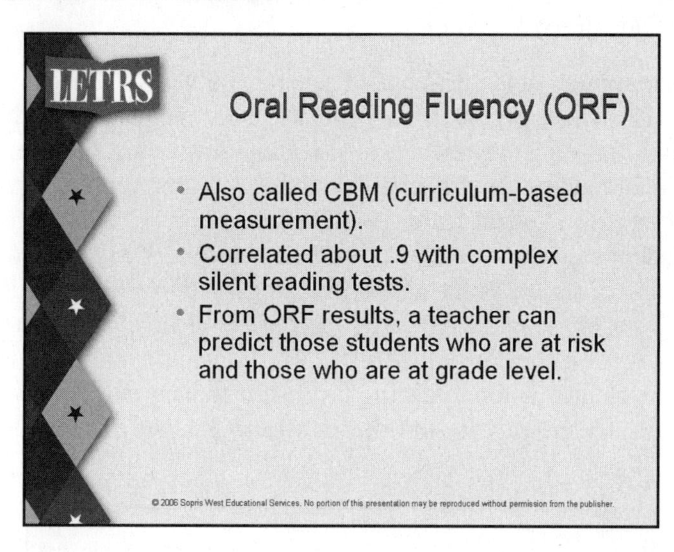

Slide 39

Oral reading fluency (ORF) assessment, also known as a form of curriculum-based measurement (CBM), has a number of advantages (Hosp & Hosp, 2003):

- ORF measures do not take much time.
- If the student is making progress, small increments of improvement are visible.
- Assessments can be used as often as every week to monitor a student's progress.

Through simple charting of their oral reading fluency, students can see that they are making progress. Results can be used to group students for instruction.

LETRS

How to Administer ORF

- Use three equivalent reading passages.
- Ask the student to orally read each passage for one minute.
- Score: WCPM (words correct per minute).
- Use passages that are at about the student's instructional reading level (approx. 95% correct) to get the score.
- Take the middle score.

Slide 40

Three, one-minute timed readings of several equivalent passages are sufficient to find an average, reliable estimate of a student's oral reading fluency. First, the student's instructional reading level must be determined. Instructional reading level is approximately 95% correct (approximately three errors if the student reads 55–60 WCPM; approximately five errors if the student reads 100 WCPM). Hosp and Hosp (2003) advise that students in first or second grade who are reading 40–60 WCPM should make four or fewer errors in a passage of appropriate difficulty, while students in grades 3–6 who are reading 70–100 WCPM should make six or fewer errors at their instructional reading level. If a student makes more errors per minute, the passage is too difficult (also known as the frustration level).

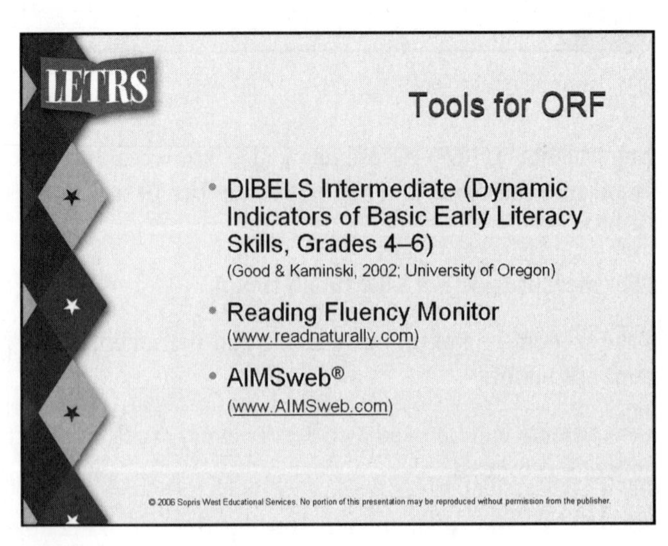

Slide 41

Three available tools for administering a timed test of oral reading are listed below:

- DIBELS Intermediate (Dynamic Indicators of Basic Early Literacy Skills, Grades 4–6) (Good & Kaminski, 2002) (dibels.uoregon.edu; Sopris West Educational Services: www.sopriswest.com)
- Reading Fluency Monitor (www.readnaturally.com)
- AIMSweb® (www.AIMSweb.com)

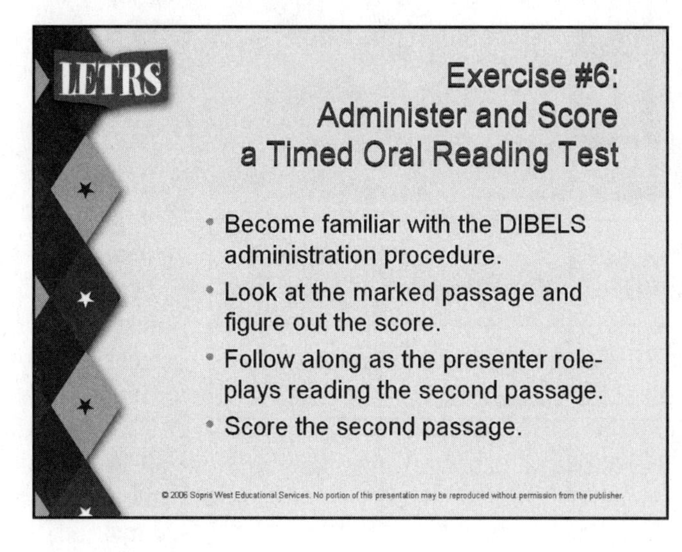

Slide 42

Exercise #6: Administer and Score a Timed Oral Reading Test

Name: ____________________ Teacher: ____________________

School: ____________________ District: ____________________

DIBELS®

6th Edition

	Benchmark 1 Beginning/Fall	Benchmark 2 Middle/Winter	Benchmark 3 End/Spring
Date			
DIBELS Oral Reading Fluency	(middle score)	(middle score)	(middle score)
Retell Fluency (Optional)	(middle score)	(middle score)	(middle score)

Fifth Grade Scoring Booklet
Benchmark Assessment

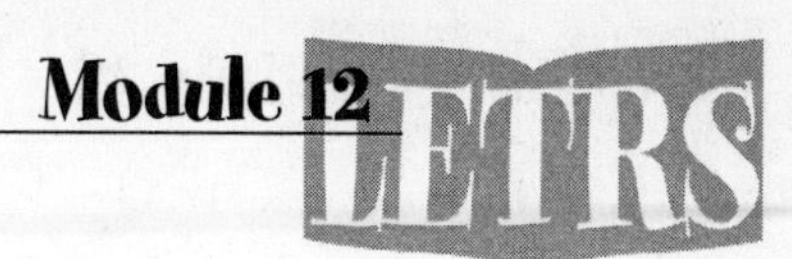

Exercise #6: Administer and Score a Timed Oral Reading Test (continued)

DIBELS® Oral Reading Fluency

Short Form Directions

Make sure you have reviewed the long form of the directions and have them available. Say these specific directions to the student:

Please read this (point) ***out loud. If you get stuck, I will tell you the word so you can keep reading. When I say "Stop," I may ask you to tell me about what you read, so do your best reading. Start here*** (point to the first word of the passage). ***Begin.***

Start your stopwatch when the student says the first word of the passage.

At the end of **1 minute**, place a bracket (**]**) after the last word provided by the student, stop and reset the stopwatch, and say, ***"Stop."*** (remove the passage)

If the student reads more than 10 words correct, proceed with the retell part. Say,

Please tell me all about what you just read. Try to tell me everything you can. Begin. Start your stopwatch after you say "Begin."

The first time the student does not say anything for 3 seconds, say, ***"Try to tell me everything you can."*** This prompt can be used only once.

If the student does not say anything or gets off track for 5 seconds, circle the total number of words in the student's retell and say, ***"Stop."***

At the end of **1 minute**, circle the total number of words in the student's retell and say, ***"Stop."***

Reminder

Discontinue rule—No words read correctly in the first row.

Hesitation rule—3 seconds—Tell the student the word. If necessary, indicate for student to continue with next word.

Do not give passages #2 and #3 and do not administer retell if student reads fewer than 10 words correctly.

Exercise #6: Administer and Score a Timed Oral Reading Test (continued)

Benchmark 3.2
DIBELS® Oral Reading Fluency

Whale Song

I live with my cousin, Jackson, who is a marine biologist. His	12
job is to study the "conversations" that the whales have with	23
each other. Jackson says the sounds these wondrous creatures	32
make are really like singing. If you visit our house, you will hear	45
these songs playing on our stereo more than any other kind of	57
music.	58
These haunting songs have been described as creaks, groans,	67
moans, chirps, whistles, and squeaks. The songs are not just	77
sounds, but are really melodies with a beginning, middle, and	87
end. A whale will repeat the same song over and over, but slowly	100
the song changes over time and every few years, new songs	111
appear.	112
Humpback whales are found throughout the world. Males	120
from the same area sing similar melodies. Just like you can	131
sometimes tell where people come from by listening to them	141
talk, Jackson can tell where a whale comes from by listening to	153
recordings of its song. My cousin thinks the songs are a way of	166
sharing information and creating and maintaining a social	174
community. His research examines how baby whales learn the	183
songs of their region.	187
Male humpback whales can produce songs that last for up to	198
twenty minutes—the longest of all animals. Scuba divers who	208
hold their breath so they won't make any noise, and swimmers	219
who are least ten feet below the surface, can hear the whales. To	232
get a really good recording of the songs, you must lower a	244
special microphone into the sea and be pretty close.	253

Page 18

Exercise #6: Administer and Score a Timed Oral Reading Test (continued)

Whale Song (Continued)

People have been recording these amazing whale songs for	262
over thirty years. Next time you are in a music store, ask to listen	276
to recording of a humpback whale and you won't believe your	287
ears! At first I thought the songs were pretty strange. The more I	300
listened, the more I liked them. Now I almost think I understand	312
how the whale was feeling.	317

Retell: ORF Total:________

⊗ • • • • • • • • • * • • • • • • • • • * • • • • • • • • • *	30
⊗ • • • • • • • • • * • • • • • • • • • * • • • • • • • • • *	60
⊗ • • • • • • • • • * • • • • • • • • • * • • • • • • • • • *	90
⊗ • • • • • • • • • * • • • • • • • • • * • • • • • • • • • *	120
⊗ • • • • • • • • • * • • • • • • • • • * • • • • • • • • • *	150
⊗ • • • • • • • • • * • • • • • • • • • * • • • • • • • • • *	180

Retell Total:________

Notes:

Exercise #6: Administer and Score a Timed Oral Reading Test (continued)

Directions for Scoring—Part 1: Oral Reading Fluency

1. Score reading passages immediately after administration.
2. *Discontinue Rule.* If the student does not read any words correctly in the first row of the first passage, discontinue the task and record a score of zero (0) on the front cover.
3. Record the total number of words read correctly on the bottom of the scoring sheet for each passage.
4. If the student reads fewer than 10 words correct on the first passage, record his/her score on the front cover and do not administer passages 2 and 3.
5. If the student reads 3 passages, record his/her middle score on the front cover. For example, if the student gets scores of 27, 36, and 25, record a score of 27 on the front cover.
6. *Hesitation or Struggle With Words.* If a student hesitates or struggles with a word for 3 seconds, tell the student the word and mark the word as incorrect. If necessary, indicate for the student to continue with the next word.

Passage	Student Says	Scoring Procedure	Correct Words/ Total Words
I have a goldfish.	"I have a … (3 seconds)"	I have a ~~goldfish~~.	3/4

7. *Hyphenated Words.* Hyphenated words count as two words if both parts can stand alone as individual words. Hyphenated words count as one word if either part cannot stand alone as an individual word.

Passage	Number of Words
I gave Ben a red yo-yo.	6
We did push-ups, pull-ups, and sit-ups.	9

8. *Numerals.* Numerals must be read correctly in the context of the sentence.

Passage	Student Says	Scoring Procedure	Correct Words/ Total Words
My father is 36.	"My father is thirty-six."	My father is 36.	4/4
My father is 36.	"My father is three six."	My father is ~~36~~.	3/4
I am 6 years old.	"I am six years old."	I am 6 years old.	5/5

Exercise #6: Administer and Score a Timed Oral Reading Test (continued)

9. *Mispronounced Words.* A word is scored as correct if it is pronounced correctly in the context of the sentence. If the word is mispronounced in the context, it is scored as an error.

Passage	Student Says	Scoring Procedure	Correct Words/ Total Words
It was a live fish.	"It was a liv fish" (i.e., with a short "i").	It was a ~~live~~ fish.	4/5
I ate too much.	"I eat too much."	I ~~ate~~ too much.	3/4

10. *Self-Corrections.* A word is scored as correct if it is initially mispronounced but the student self-corrects within 3 seconds. Mark "SC" above the word and score as correct.

Passage	Student Says	Scoring Procedure	Correct Words/ Total Words
It was a live fish.	"It was a liv … live fish" (i.e., self-corrects to long "i" within 3 sec.).	SC It was a ~~live~~ fish.	5/5

11. *Repeated Words.* Words that are repeated are not scored as incorrect and are ignored in scoring.

Passage	Student Says	Scoring Procedure	Correct Words/ Total Words
I have a goldfish.	"I have a … I have a goldfish."	I have a goldfish.	4/4

12. *Articulation and Dialect.* The student is not penalized for imperfect pronunciation due to dialect, articulation, or second-language interference. For example, if the student *consistently* says /th/ for /s/, and reads "rest" as "retht," he or she should be given credit for a correct word. This is a professional judgment and should be based on the student's responses and any prior knowledge of his/her speech patterns.

Passage	Student Says	Scoring Procedure	Correct Words/ Total Words
It is time for a rest.	"It is time for a retht." (articulation)	It is time for a rest.	6/6
We took the short cut.	"We took the shot cut." (dialect)	We took the short cut.	5/5

13. *Inserted Words.* Inserted words are ignored and not counted as errors. The student also does not get additional credit for inserted words. If the student frequently inserts extra words, note the pattern at the bottom of the scoring page.

Passage	Student Says	Scoring Procedure	Correct Words/ Total Words
It is time for a rest.	"It is time for a long rest."	It is time for a rest.	6/6
I ate too much.	"I ate way too much."	I ate too much.	4/4

Exercise #6: Administer and Score a Timed Oral Reading Test (continued)

14. *Omitted Words.* Omitted words are scored as incorrect.

Passage	Student Says	Scoring Procedure	Correct Words/ Total Words
It is time for a rest.	"It is time for rest."	It is time for ~~a~~ rest.	5/6
I ate too much.	"I ate much."	I ate ~~too~~ much.	3/4

15. *Word Order.* All words that are read correctly but in the wrong order are scored as incorrect.

Passage	Student Says	Scoring Procedure	Correct Words/ Total Words
The ice cream man comes.	"The cream ice man comes."	The ~~ice~~ ~~cream~~ man comes.	3/5
I ate too much.	"I too ate much."	I ~~ate~~ ~~too~~ much.	2/4

16. *Abbreviations.* Abbreviations should be read in the way you would normally pronounce the abbreviation in conversation. For example, TV could be read as "teevee" or "television," but Mr. would be read as "mister."

Passage	Student Says	Scoring Procedure	Correct Words/ Total Words
May I watch TV?	"May I watch teevee?"	May I watch TV?	4/4
May I watch TV?	"May I watch television?"	May I watch TV?	4/4
My teacher is Mr. Smith.	"My teacher is Mister Smith."	My teacher is Mr. Smith.	5/5
My teacher is Mr. Smith.	"My teacher is 'm' 'r' Smith."	My teacher is ~~Mr.~~ Smith.	4/5

Directions for Scoring—Part 2: Retell Fluency

1. Score retell while the child is responding. Circle total number of words immediately after examiner says, "Stop."

2. *Number of Retell Words.* Count the number of words the child retells that illustrates his/her understanding of the passage.

3. *Exclamations are not counted.* Only actual words are counted. If the child inserts mazes or other sounds, inserted sounds are not counted.

Passage	Student Says
I love going to the library downtown. There are so many books. There is a big room in the library that is just for kids. I can reach all the books by myself.	They uhh they are going to the uhhh library. It is uhhh downtown. uhh There's a room.

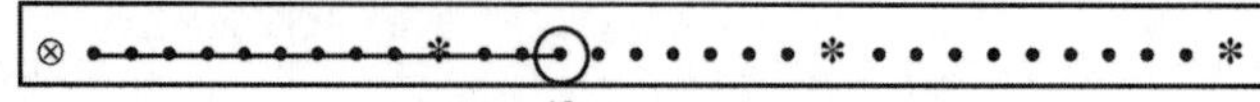
13

Exercise #6: Administer and Score a Timed Oral Reading Test (continued)

4. <u>*Count contractions as one word.*</u> For example, if the child uses "She's" or "We'll," they would only count as one word.

Passage	Student Says
I love going to the library downtown. There are so many books. There is a big room in the library that is just for kids. I can reach all the books by myself.	They're going to the library. It's downtown. There's a room.

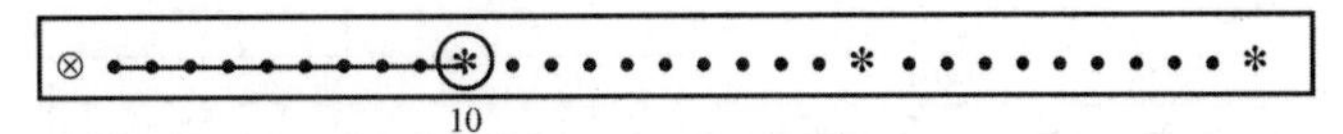

5. *Songs or recitations are not included.* If the child recites the ABCs or tells a song or poem, even if relevant to the retell, the recitation, song, or poem is not counted.

Passage	Student Says
I love going to the library downtown. There are so many books. There is a big room in the library that is just for kids. I can reach all the books by myself.	They're going to the library. The books have letters like A B C D E F G H I J K L M N O P Q R S T U V W X Y Z.

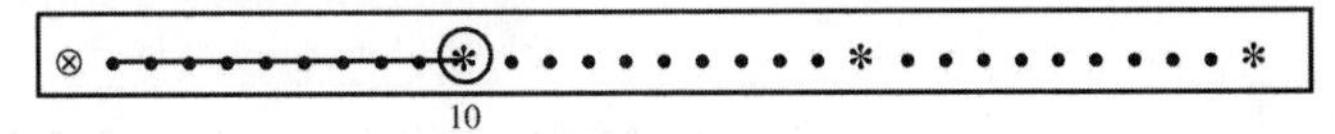

6. *Minor repetitions, redundancies, irrelevancies, and inaccuracies are counted.* The crucial judgment is whether the student is retelling the passage or has gotten off track on another story or topic. In this example, the child (1) goes from "they" to "I", (2) changes "love" to "like," (3) changes the order of events, (4) repeats "library," (5) confuses "room" and "books," and (6) confuses "reach" and "read." However, her retell is fundamentally on track, and all words would count.

Passage	Student Says
I love going to the library downtown. There are so many books. There is a big room in the library that is just for kids. I can reach all the books by myself.	They're going to the library. The library is downtown. I like the library. They have books just for kids. I can read them myself

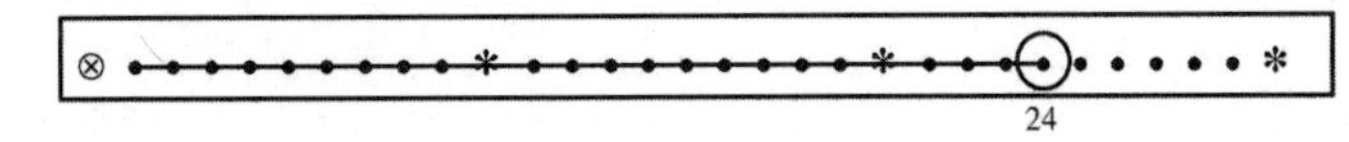

7. *Rote repetitions of words or phrases are not counted.*

Passage	Student Says
I love going to the library downtown. There are so many books. There is a big room in the library that is just for kids. I can reach all the books by myself.	(sing-song voice) They're going to the library. They're going to the library. They're going to the library.

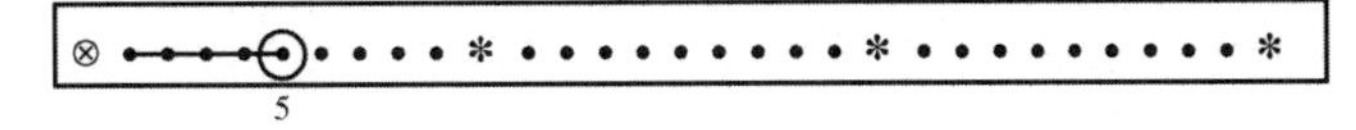

Exercise #6: Administer and Score a Timed Oral Reading Test (continued)

8. *Repeating their retell is not counted.* Especially when children are prompted to "try to tell me everything you can," they may simply repeat what they have already provided.

Passage	Student Says
I love going to the library downtown. There are so many books. There is a big room in the library that is just for kids. I can reach all the books by myself.	They're going to the library. Lots of books. [prompt] They're going to the library. Books.

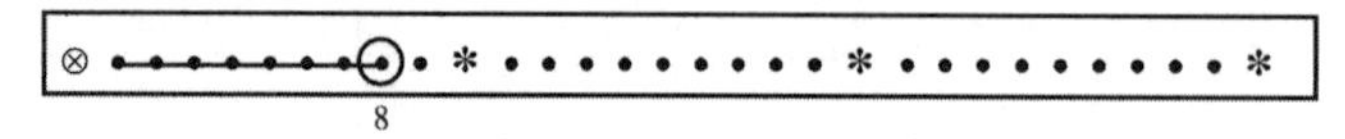

9. *Stories or irrelevancies that are off track are not counted.* Children may start telling something from their own experience that is vaguely related to the passage. Such stories are not counted.

Passage	Student Says
I love going to the library downtown. There are so many books. There is a big room in the library that is just for kids. I can reach all the books by myself.	They're going to the library. They have lots of books. My mom took me to the library. We got Dr. Seuss and *Willy Wonka.* They are my favorite books.

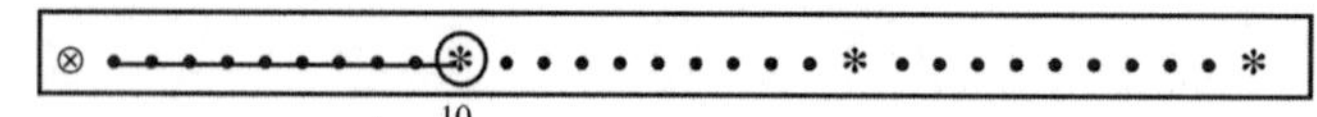

Exercise #6: Administer and Score a Timed Oral Reading Test (continued)

Benchmark 3.2
DIBELS® Oral Reading Fluency

Whale Song

I live with my cousin, Jackson, who is a marine biologist. His 12
job is to study the "conversations" that the whales have with 23
each other. Jackson says the sounds these wondrous creatures 32
make are really like singing. If you visit our house, you will hear 45
these songs playing on our stereo more than any other kind of 57
music. 58

These haunting songs have been described as creaks, groans, 67
moans, chirps, whistles, and squeaks. The songs are not just 77
sounds, but are really melodies with a beginning, middle, and 87
end. A whale will repeat the same song over and over, but slowly 100
the song changes over time and every few years, new songs 111
appear. 112

Humpback whales are found throughout the world. Males 120
from the same area sing similar melodies. Just like you can 131
sometimes tell where people come from by listening to them 141
talk, Jackson can tell where a whale comes from by listening to 153
recordings of its song. My cousin thinks the songs are a way of 166
sharing information and creating and maintaining a social 174
community. His research examines how baby whales learn the 183
songs of their region. 187

Male humpback whales can produce songs that last for up to 198
twenty minutes—the longest of all animals. Scuba divers who 208
hold their breath so they won't make any noise, and swimmers 219
who are least ten feet below the surface, can hear the whales. To 232
get a really good recording of the songs, you must lower a 244
special microphone into the sea and be pretty close. 253

Page 18

Exercise #6: Administer and Score a Timed Oral Reading Test (continued)

Whale Song (Continued)

People have been recording these amazing whale songs for	262
over thirty years. Next time you are in a music store, ask to listen	276
to recording of a humpback whale and you won't believe your	287
ears! At first I thought the songs were pretty strange. The more I	300
listened, the more I liked them. Now I almost think I understand	312
how the whale was feeling.	317

ORF Total:_________

Retell:

⊗ • • • • • • • • • • * • • • • • • • • • • * • • • • • • • • • • *	30
⊗ • • • • • • • • • • * • • • • • • • • • • * • • • • • • • • • • *	60
⊗ • • • • • • • • • • * • • • • • • • • • • * • • • • • • • • • • *	90
⊗ • • • • • • • • • • * • • • • • • • • • • * • • • • • • • • • • *	120
⊗ • • • • • • • • • • * • • • • • • • • • • * • • • • • • • • • • *	150
⊗ • • • • • • • • • • * • • • • • • • • • • * • • • • • • • • • • *	180

Retell Total:_________

Notes:

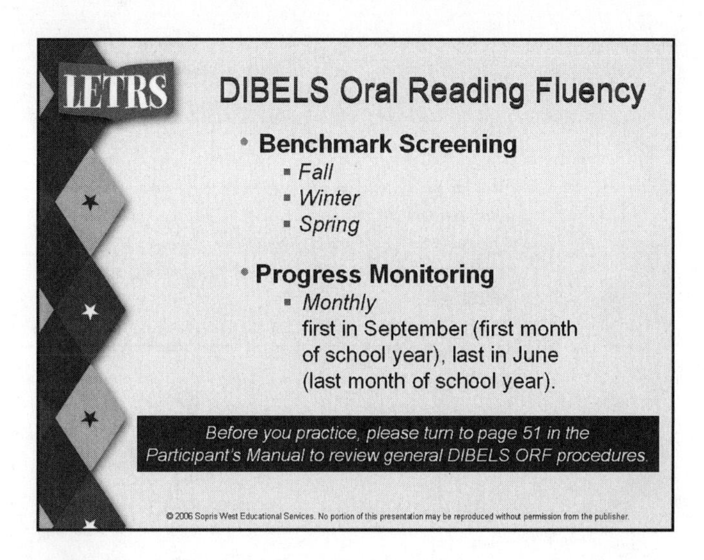

Slide 43

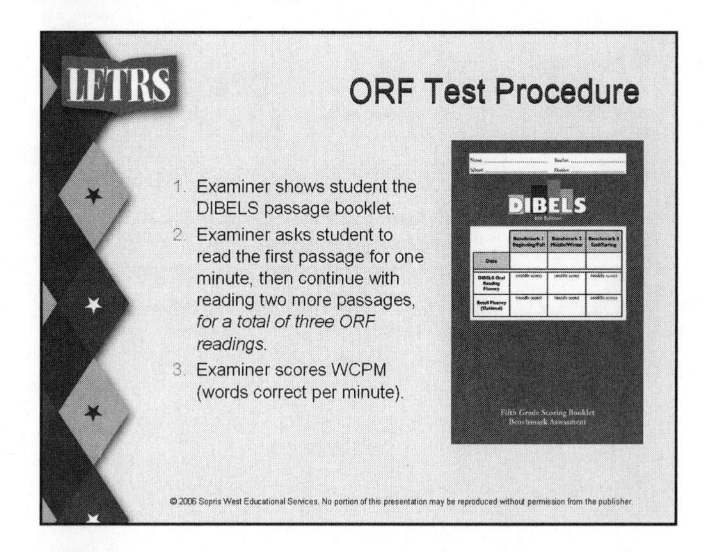

Slide 44

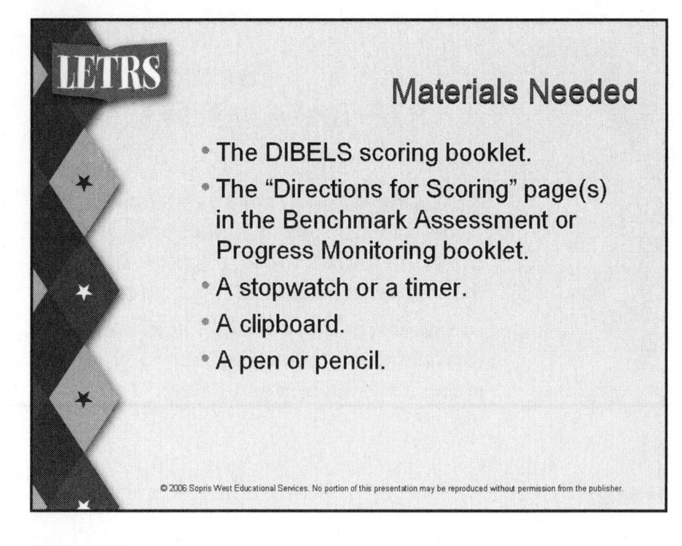

Slide 45

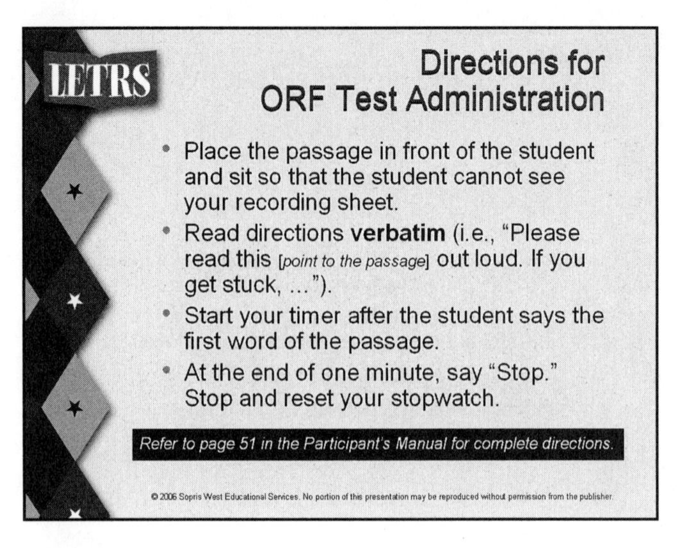

Slide 46

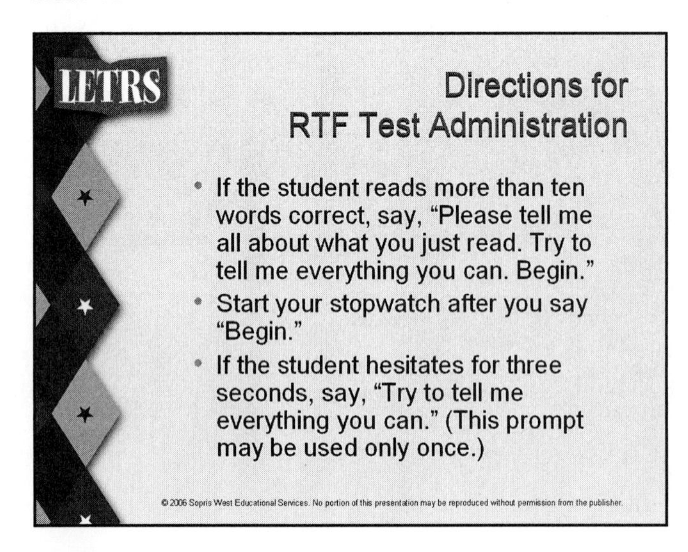

Slide 47

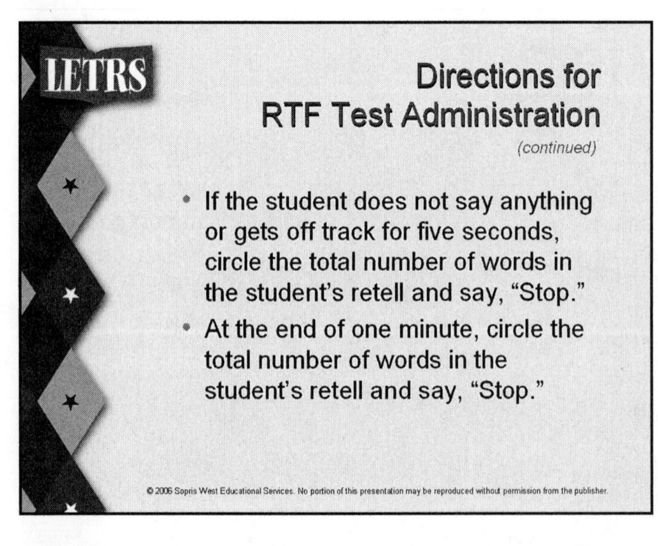

Slide 48

LETRS

Directions for Marking the Booklet

- Draw a slash (/) through each word read incorrectly.
- Draw a bracket ( ]) after the last word read correctly at the end of the minute.

Slide 49

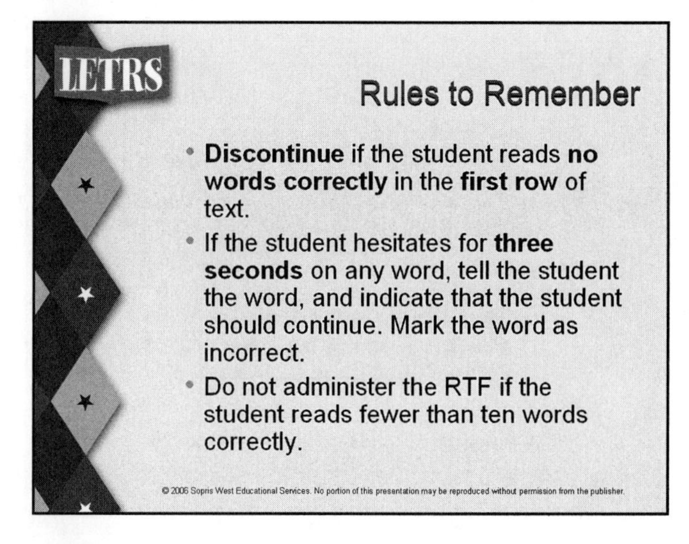

Slide 50

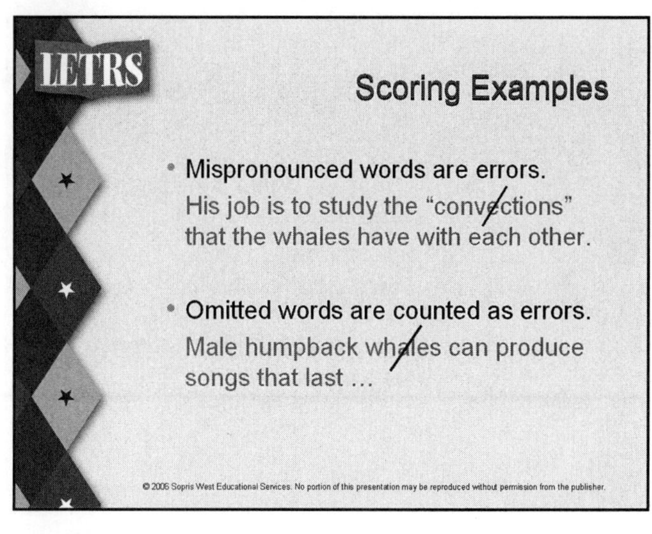

Slide 51

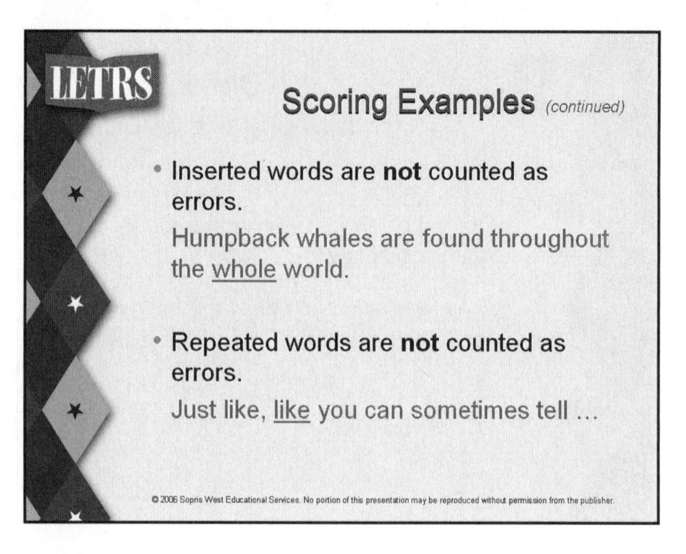

Slide 52

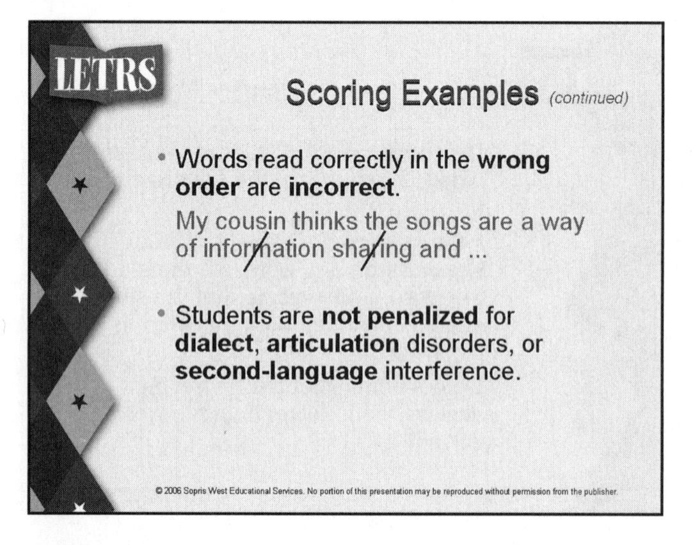

Slide 53

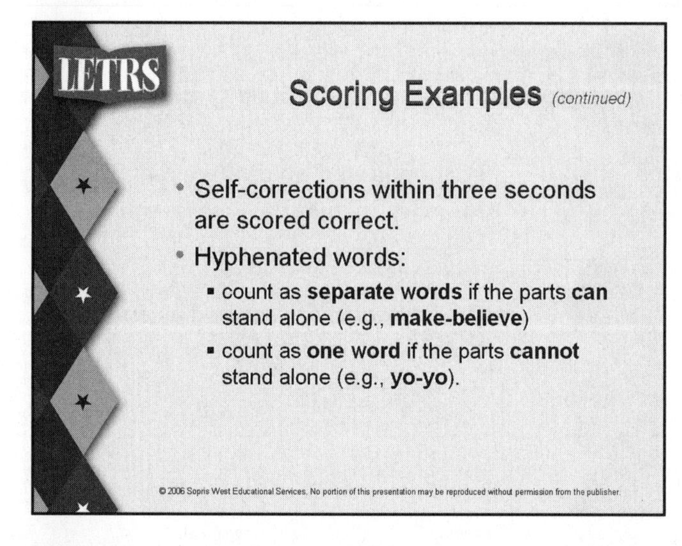

Slide 54

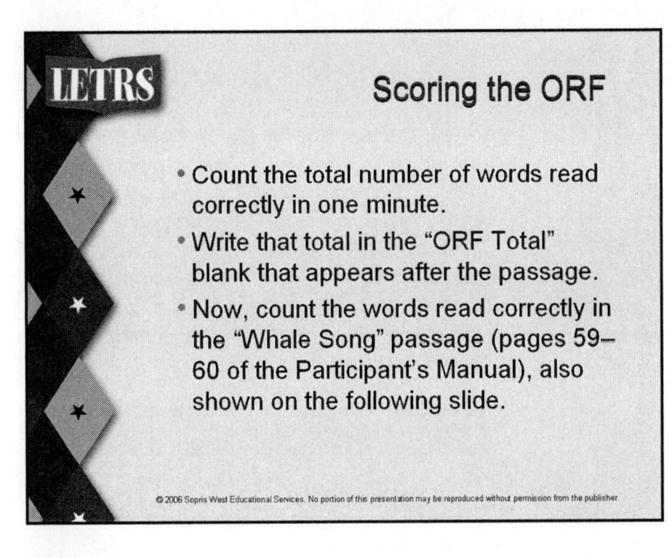

Slide 55

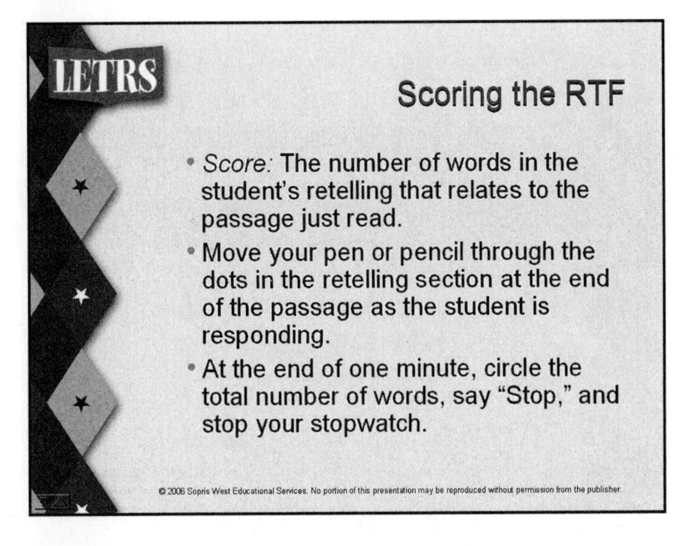

Slide 56

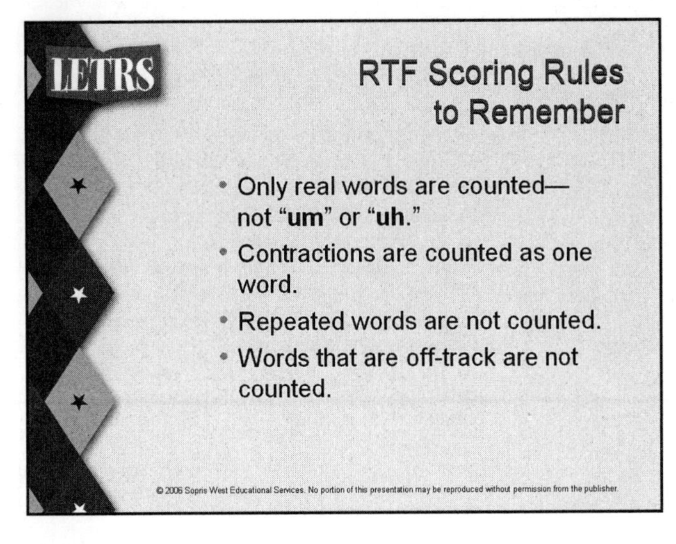

Slide 57

LETRS

Example of RTF of "Whale Song"

"Well, the humpbacks like to sing songs under the water. They sound like creaks and moans, but they are really real songs. Um, the songs are special to each whale, you know, like they can tell where the whale comes from by its song. Sometimes they are 20 minutes long. I'd like to get a record of whale songs."

Use the Retell scoring template on page 60 in the Participant's Manual to score this RTF.

Slide 58

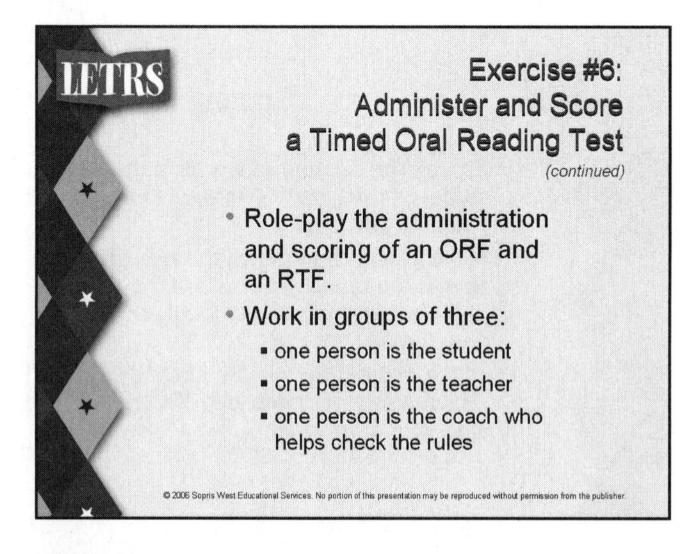

Slide 59

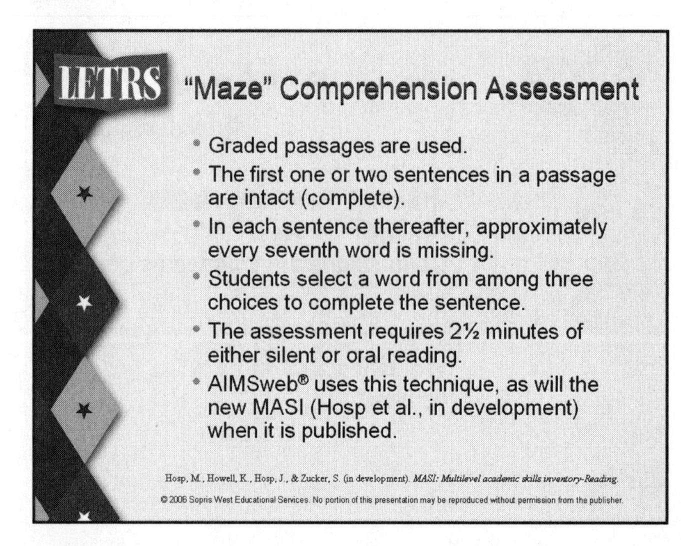

Slide 60

Comprehension Assessment

Timed oral passage reading should always include a comprehension component, such as answering questions, retelling the main ideas, or summarizing the passage. Otherwise, students may equate reading fast with reading well. DIBELS, for example, asks the student to retell the passage just read. The Retelling Fluency (RTF) score of DIBELS is based on the number of relevant words in the student's retelling.

Another method for estimating comprehension that has been used successfully in research is called the "maze" method (Deno et al., 2001; Hosp, Howell, Hosp, & Zucker, in development). The student reads a passage, out loud or silently, in which approximately every seventh word is deleted. Then, the student must select one of three possible replacement words to restore the meaning of the text. The number of correct replacements found in 2.5 minutes of reading is the index for comprehension on maze passages. The correlation between maze format tests and oral reading fluency measures (WCPM) is very high, and the results of the two kinds of measures correspond closely. AIMSweb® includes a comprehension-testing component that uses maze passages.

The following example is from *MASI: Multilevel Academic Skills Inventory-Reading* (Hosp et al., in development).

Student Maze Passage, Level 3B[4]

News

Who writes what you read in the newspaper? Reporters write stories about things that are

happening in your city. There are other reporters ____________ live in other
1. (among, newspapers, who)

cities. ____________ write about what is ____________ in their cities.
2. (They, Extra, Squirrels) 3. (happening, message, pointing)

A ____________ who is far away ____________ write a news story ____________ send
4. (city, reporter, that) 5. (did, can, business) 6. (and, but, reporter)

it "over the ____________." When you make a ____________ call, your voice goes
7. (far, books, Internet) 8. (write, telephone, cooking)

"____________ the wire." The reporter's ____________ is sent about the ____________
9. (over, until, other) 10. (news, city, some) 11. (new, same, get)

way. The telephone line ____________ the signals. Large machines ____________
12. (special, happens, carries) 13. (comic, receive, go)

the signals. They type ____________ the story the reporter ____________. You do not
14. (out, but, call) 15. (everyone, lived, wrote)

have ____________ wait very long to ____________ out what's happening anywhere ____________
16. (to, in, other) 17. (find, write, in) 18. (wire, for, in)

your world. Of course, ____________ newspaper pays to get ____________ "over
19. (your, dark, with) 20. (machine, news, around)

the wire." Reporters ____________ not only people ____________ write what you read
21. (are, can, story) 22. (can, they, who)

____________ the paper. Your friends ____________ neighbors write letters to
23. (in, before, news) 24. (some, for, and)

____________ newspaper. These letters tell ____________ those people think about
25. (the, and, line) 26. (cities, what, every)

[4] Provided by and used with permission of Ken Howell.

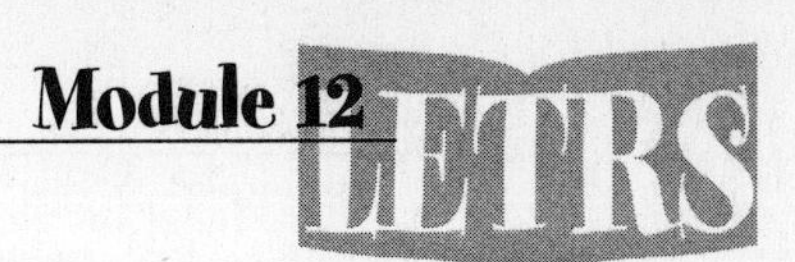

________________ in the news. Some ________________ are printed in the
27. (events, wires, pays) 28. (also, voices, letters)

______________________ so everyone can read ________________. They are usually
29. (newspaper, telephone, and) 30. (signals, them, pays)

printed ______________ a special page called ____________ editorial page. What about
31. (early, about, on) 32. (same, in, the)

____________ "funny papers"? Special writers _______________ and draw the
33. (the, and, call) 34. (line, write, paper)

comic ______________________. Newspapers buy their work ___________ that people
35. (strips, telephones, answer) 36. (in, wait, so)

will buy ______________ newspaper. There are many _________________ writers who
37. (also, button, the) 38. (other, long, carries)

work for _______________ newspaper. Some write about __________________ or books
39. (the, on, everyone) 40. (in, afternoons, movies)

or shows. ____________________ write about cooking or ______________________. Some
41. (Some, Voices, Special) 42. (begin, bowls, gardening)

write about sports. Some even make up the crossword puzzles! Would you like to write

for a newspaper?

Teacher Scoring Sheet for Maze Passage, Level 3B

MATERIALS: Student Maze Passages, Level 3B; teacher scoring sheets; pen or pencil.

BASAL: Start with the first sentence.

CEILING: Stop students after 2½ minutes.

SCORING: Circle each student's choices for the missing words. Correct answers are in **boldface** CAPITAL letters.

NOTES: If a student stops working or skips an item, remind the student to finish all items.

DIRECTIONS: Point to the passage and say:

> *"When I say 'Please begin,' I want you to read this story to yourself. You will have 2½ minutes to read the story and circle your answers. Remember, some of the words in the story are missing. In their place is a blank. Under the blank are three words. You are to choose the one word that makes sense in the story. Remember, only one word is correct. Any questions? (Pause.) Please begin."*

After 2½ minutes, tell students to stop.

Answer Key for Maze Passage, Level 3B ("News")

1. among, newspapers, **WHO**
2. **THEY**, Extra, Squirrels
3. **HAPPENING**, message, pointing — # Correct: _____
4. city, **REPORTER**, that
5. did, **CAN**, business
6. **AND**, but, reporter
7. far, books, **INTERNET**
8. write, **TELEPHONE**, cooking
9. **OVER**, until, other
10. **NEWS**, city, some
11. new, **SAME**, get
12. special, happens, **CARRIES** — # Correct: _____
13. comic, **RECEIVE**, go

14. **OUT**, but, call
15. everyone, lived, **WROTE**
16. **TO**, in, other
17. **FIND**, write, in
18. wire, for, **IN**
19. **YOUR**, dark, with
20. machine, **NEWS**, around — # Correct: _____
21. **ARE**, can, story
22. can, they, **WHO**
23. **IN**, before, news
24. some, for, **AND**
25. **THE**, and, line
26. cities, **WHAT**, every
27. **EVENTS**, wires, pays
28. also, voices, **LETTERS**
29. **NEWSPAPER**, telephone, and
30. signals, **THEM**, pays
31. early, about, **ON**
32. same, in, **THE** — # Correct: _____
33. **THE**, and, call
34. line, **WRITE**, paper
35. **STRIPS**, telephones, answer
36. in, wait, **SO**
37. also, button, **THE** — # Correct: _____
38. **OTHER**, long, carries
39. **THE**, on, everyone
40. in, afternoons, **MOVIES**
41. **SOME**, Voices, Special
42. begin, bowls, **GARDENING**

Total # Correct: __________

Total Errors: __________

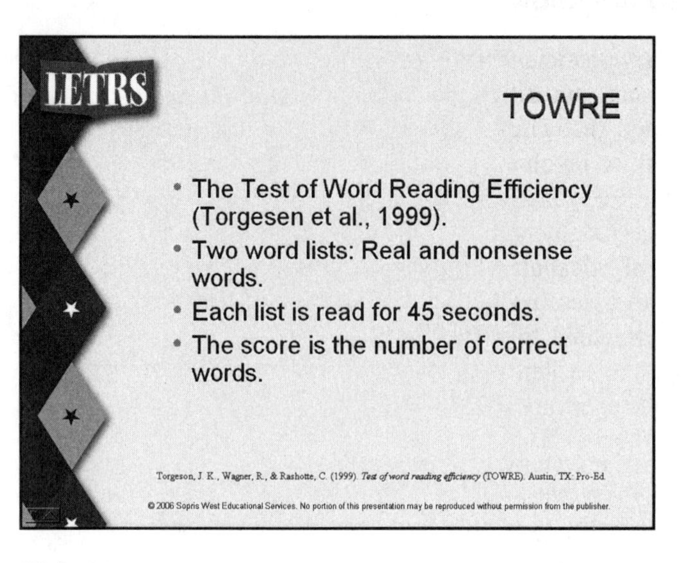

Slide 61

Word Recognition, Rate, and Accuracy

Another efficient, validated measure of word reading and phonic decoding skills is the Test of Word Reading Efficiency (TOWRE) (Torgesen, Wagner, & Rashotte, 1999). It is administered individually and includes two subtests, one of real-word reading and one of nonsense-word reading. For each list, the student is asked to read as many words as possible in 45 seconds. The research underpinnings for this simple measure are substantial; individual-word reading skill is highly correlated with passage reading fluency. However, only in oral passage reading can comprehension be evaluated as well.

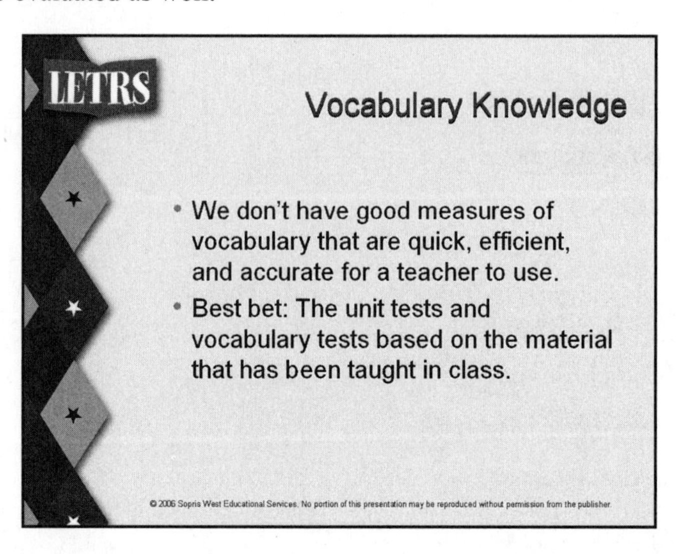

Slide 62

Vocabulary Knowledge

Vocabulary proficiency is extremely important in instruction and reading achievement, but difficult to measure. Aside from the Peabody Picture Vocabulary Test-Third Edition (PPVT-III)—which is given individually and does not involve reading—all other vocabulary measures known to us at this time require reading or a lengthy testing process that includes qualitative judgments of a student's orally given word definitions. The richness of vocabulary possessed by intermediate and older students is difficult to assess unless reading tasks are used. As a result, vocabulary assessments tend to benchmark a student's ability to decode words in multiple-choice items rather than accurately reflect the student's command and repertoire of vocabulary.

One possible strategy is to orally administer a written vocabulary test as a listening comprehension test, with the examiner reading the vocabulary words and multiple-choice responses to the student. Otherwise, tests such as the Vocabulary subtest of the Wechsler Intelligence Scale for Children–IV, which are given by psychologists or learning specialists, are the best norm-referenced measures of vocabulary at this time.

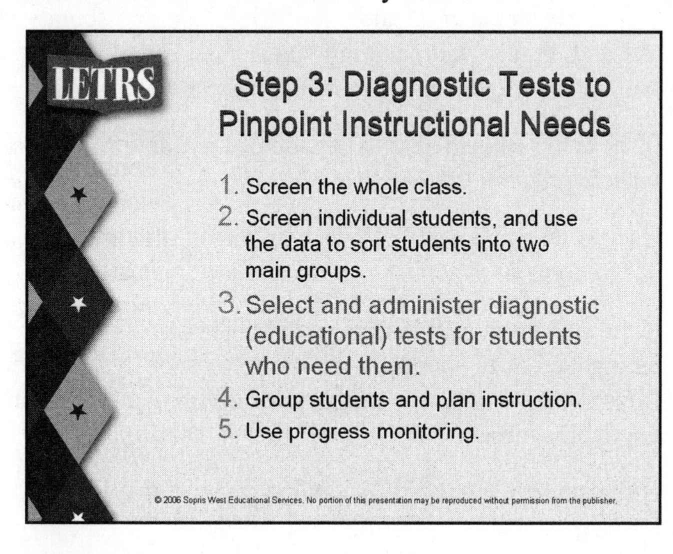

Slide 63

Step 3: Diagnostic Tests to Pinpoint Instructional Needs

Knowledge of Phonics and Syllabication

Those students who are substantially below benchmark in oral reading fluency and whose word reading is inaccurate (on a measure such as the TOWRE) should be assessed for phonics knowledge. The majority of poor readers at the intermediate level has unresolved problems with decoding and word recognition and will need instruction in word

decoding. Instructional time can be saved, however, if students' specific needs are identified. These questions should be asked and answered:

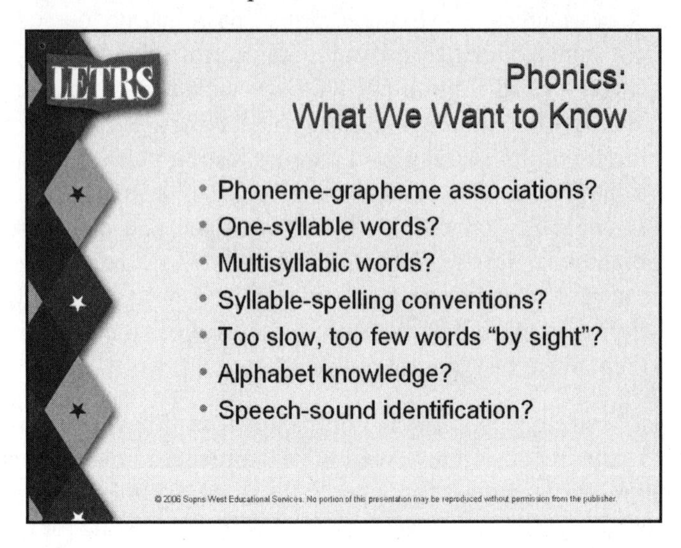

Slide 64

- Is the student accurate and automatic in naming sounds for letters and, in turn, knowing how individual sounds are typically spelled (basic phoneme-grapheme correspondences)?
- If so, is the student able to decode one-syllable real and nonsense words out of context?
- If so, is the student able to decode longer, multisyllable words out of context?
- If the student is unable to decode longer words, does he or she recognize vowel sounds in the most common syllable types? Does the student have a strategy for dividing and blending multisyllable words?
- Is the student accurate in decoding, but too slow in word reading?
- If the student is not accurate in decoding simple words, does he or she know the letter names, and can he or she produce the alphabetic sequence in the words?
- If the student is not accurate in decoding simple words, can he or she identify, pronounce, segment, blend, and manipulate individual speech sounds in the words? (Does the student have requisite phonological awareness? If not, at what level does the student need instruction?)

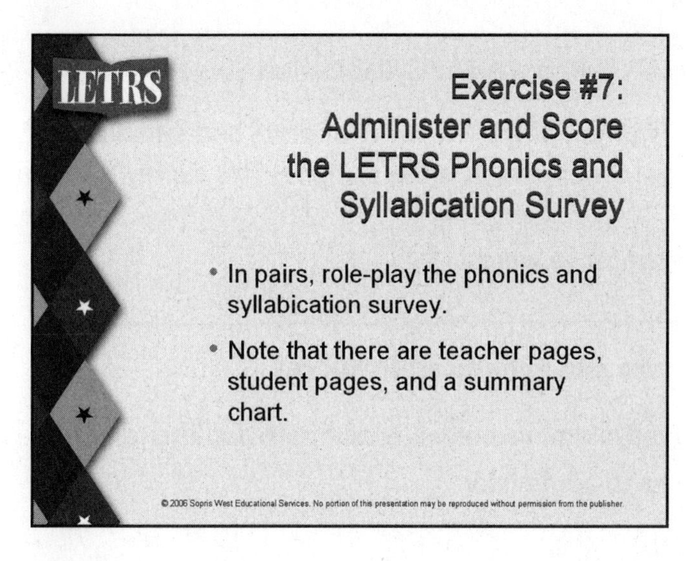
LETRS
Exercise #7:
Administer and Score
the LETRS Phonics and
Syllabication Survey
• In pairs, role-play the phonics and syllabication survey.
• Note that there are teacher pages, student pages, and a summary chart.
© 2006 Sopris West Educational Services. No portion of this presentation may be reproduced without permission from the publisher.

Slide 65

Exercise #7: Administer and Score the LETRS Phonics and Syllabication Survey

- With a partner, role-play the administration of the following phonics and syllabication survey. (One person is the tester, and the other person is the student.) This survey is untimed.
- Make sure you can pronounce the nonsense words.

The LETRS Phonics and Syllabication Survey

Directions: This survey should be individually administered. It is untimed, but intended to be brief; it should take about 10 minutes to administer.

This survey is a tool for determining which phonics correspondences and syllable spelling conventions a student can read and for isolating those correspondences and conventions that the student has yet to learn. The LETRS Phonics and Syllabication Survey is designed for poor readers in grade 3 and beyond. (A more basic, beginning-level survey, designed by Linda Farrell, is in Appendix B of this LETRS module and is recommended for younger or severely reading-disabled students.)

The series of decoding tasks is organized according to the basic syllable spelling conventions of English. Those conventions represent vowel sounds: short vowels in closed syllables, long vowels in **VCe** and many vowel team syllables, Vowel-**r** syllables, and Consonant-**le** syllables. Open syllables are not tested out of the context of multisyllable words.

If the student cannot decode words, administer the foundation tasks of naming letters, writing the alphabet, and giving sounds for letters and letter combinations. With the letters **c**, **g**, **ow**, and **oo**, more than one response is correct. Accept any correct response; you may want to ask the student to tell you another sound for these letters as well.

On subtests with nonsense words, say, "I'd like you to read some words. Some will be real and some will be nonsense. Please read the nonsense words as if they were part of a real word. Do the best you can."

If the student immediately self-corrects, count the word as correct. If the student makes an error, keep going without correcting the student. Encourage the student to move on when he or she gets "stuck" on unknown words. Discontinue the survey when the word lists become too difficult for the student to read. (In this survey, good readers can read all of the phonics patterns and recognize the words with 90% or better accuracy.)

This survey should help you determine if the student needs a structured language program such as *LANGUAGE!* ® (Greene, 2005), Wilson Language Training (www.wilsonlanguage.com), SpellRead P.A.T.® (www.spellread.com/a/publish/homepage.shtml), Orton-Gillingham (www.ortonacademy.org), or *Spellography* (Moats & Rosow, 2002).

LETRS Phonics and Syllabication Survey

Student Pages

Student_____________________________Grade/Class__________ Date_____________

A. Name these letters:

y u x j w d z b n g

B. Write the alphabet in sequence:

____

____

____

____

C. Say the sound(s) each letter or letter combination represents:

g qu r j v d w dge

a e i u o

oa ee igh ay ow oy ai oo

D. Read these words. There are real words and nonsense words in this list.

rot	wed	bun	lap	kit	sum
lom	mis	pez	gom	rad	jun
napkin	weblog	rotten	unmet	cupful	Wisconsin

E. Read these words. There are real words and nonsense words in this list.

thatch	shred	chill	stomp	trust	frank
chonk	thremp	plass	bling	steck	culf
skimming	backdrop	upchuck	webcast	maddest	subject

F. Read these words. There are real and nonsense words in this list.

dome	plate	tune	vote	chime	whale
lete	pruce	wabe	pire	throme	bline
entwine	compete	implode	unmade	insane	commune

G. Read these words. There are real words and nonsense words in this list.

fur	or	yurt	girl	chard	jerk
jer	thir	zor	gurt	sarm	glers
setter	doctor	artwork	platform	surfer	starburst

H. Read these words. There are real words and nonsense words in this list.

ray	keel	bread	stew	shoal	flight
voy	wain	loob	cruit	plaud	wright
sustain	turmoil	cheater	coleslaw	soupspoon	snowboard

I. Read these words. There are real words and nonsense words in this list.

price	guard	sledge	clutch	gem	cyst
gyre	trece	woge	datch	zudge	cim

J. Read these words.

bugle	stable	battle	juggle	steeple
boggle	scrabble	maple	noodle	chortle

K. Read these words.

mittens	crushes	puffed	unknowing	evenly
dodged	poorly	frightening	breezes	guppies

L. Read these words.

something	than	would	which	until	through	
what	some	other	of	my	from	do
very	to	want	buy	friend	where	
were	because	really	know	their	every	

LETRS Phonics and Syllabication Survey

Administration and Scoring Recording Sheet

Student________________________________ Grade/Class___________ Date_______________

A. Letter Names

y u x j w d z b n g ___/10

B. Write the alphabet in sequence. ___/26

(Score: The number of letters correctly formed in the correct sequence.)

C. Letter Sounds

Consonants: g qu r j v d w dge ___/8

(If the student says /j/ for the letter g, ask for the other sound the letter represents.)

Short vowels: a e i u o ___/5

(If the student says the long vowel sound, ask for the short vowel sound.)

Vowel teams: oa ee igh ay ow oy ai oo ___/8

(The vowel team **ow** can be pronounced /ou/ [as in **cow**] or /ō/ [as in **snow**];
the vowel team **oo** can be pronounced /ū/ [as in **food**] or /ŏŏ/ [as in **book**].)

D. Closed Syllables (short vowel, simple)

Real: rot wed bun lap kit sum ___/6

Nonsense: lom mis pez gom rad jun ___/6

Combined: napkin weblog rotten unmet cupful Wisconsin ___/6

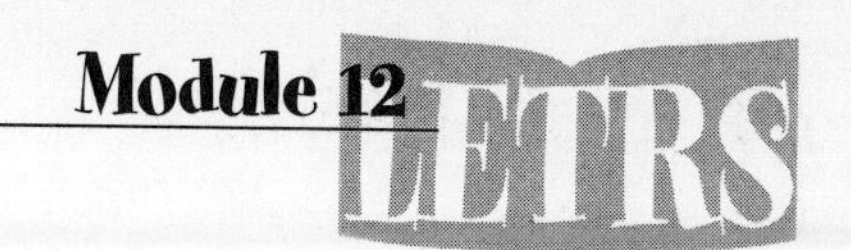

E. Closed Syllables (short vowel, complex, with digraphs and blends)

Real:	thatch shred chill stomp trust frank	___/6
Nonsense:	chonk thremp plass bling steck culf	___/6
Combined:	skimming backdrop upchuck webcast maddest subject	___/6

F. Vowel-Consonant-**e** Syllables (silent **e** or "magic" **e**)

Real:	dome plate tune vote chime whale	___/6
Nonsense:	lete pruce wabe pire throme bline	___/6
Combined:	entwine compete implode unmade insane commune	___/6

G. Vowel-**r** Syllables

Real:	fur or yurt girl chard jerk	___/6
Nonsense:	jer thir zor gurt sarm glers	___/6
Combined:	setter doctor artwork platform surfer starburst	___/6

H. Vowel Team Syllables

Real:	ray keel bread stew shoal flight	___/6
Nonsense:	voy wain loob cruit plaud wright	___/6
Combined:	sustain turmoil cheater coleslaw soupspoon snowboard	___/6

I. Complex Consonant Patterns (hard/soft **c** and **g**; **-dge**, **-tch**)

Real:	price guard sledge clutch gem cyst	___/6
Nonsense:	gyre trece woge datch zudge cim	___/6

J. Mixed Syllables With Consonant-**le**

bugle	stable	battle	juggle	steeple	
boggle	scrabble	maple	noodle	chortle	____/10

K. Base Words With Inflections and Common Suffixes

mittens	crushes	puffed	unknowing	evenly	
dodged	poorly	frightening	breezes	guppies	____/10

L. High-Frequency, Irregular Words

something	than	would	which	until	through		
what	some	other	of	my	from	do	
very	to	want	buy	friend	where		
were	because	really	know	their	every		____/25

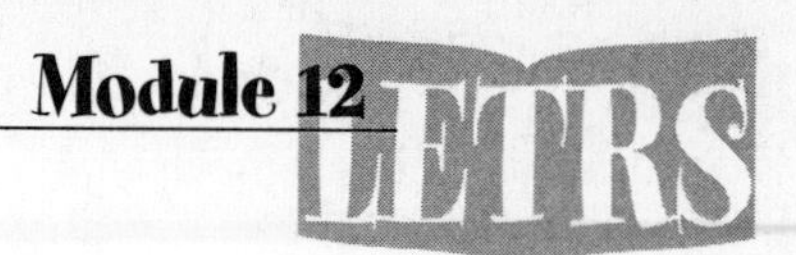

LETRS Phonics and Syllabication Survey

Summary Chart

Foundation Skill				TOTALS Pretest	TOTALS Posttest
A. Letter Names				____/10	____/10
B. Alphabet Writing				____/26	____/26
C. Letter Sounds				____/21	____/21
Phonics Skill	**Real Words**	**Nonsense Words**	**Combined Syllables**	**TOTALS Pretest**	**TOTALS Posttest**
D. Closed Syllables (short vowel, simple)	____/6	____/6	____/6	____/18	____/18
E. Closed Syllables (short vowels, complex, with digraphs and blends)	____/6	____/6	____/6	____/18	____/18
F. Vowel-Consonant-**e** Syllables	____/6	____/6	____/6	____/18	____/18
G. Vowel-**r** Syllables	____/6	____/6	____/6	____/18	____/18
H. Vowel Team Syllables	____/6	____/6	____/6	____/18	____/18
I. Complex Consonant Patterns	____/6	____/6		____/12	____/12
J. Mixed Syllables With Consonant-**le**				____/10	____/10
K. Base Words With Inflections and Common Suffixes				____/10	____/10
L. High-Frequency, Irregular Words				____/25	____/25

Narrative summary, student instructional needs:

____

____

____

____

____

____

The LETRS Survey of Morphological Knowledge

The following brief survey first samples a student's ability to recognize meaningful parts of words (morphemes) and to distinguish prefixes, roots, and suffixes. Next, the survey addresses a student's ability to read words with the most common inflectional suffixes and several basic derivational suffixes (e.g., **-s**, **-ed**, **-ful**, **-ly**, **-less**). Finally, this survey samples a student's recognition of words constructed from Latin and Greek roots, prefixes, and suffixes—words that are typically known by students in the intermediate grades.

This informal survey is not scored, as its predictive value is unknown. The survey should help teachers become aware that meaningful word parts can and should be taught directly with a program that emphasizes morphology, such as Ebbers' (2003) *Vocabulary Through Morphemes*, Henry's (2003) *Unlocking Literacy*, or the word study program *Spellography* (Moats & Rosow, 2002). Many more prefixes, roots, and suffixes than those in this survey would be part of a comprehensive word study program.

LETRS Survey of Morphological Knowledge[5]

Student Response Sheet

1. In the words below, circle the prefixes, underline the roots or base words, and box the suffixes. Some words may have no prefix or suffix, or more than one suffix. For example:

prevent	testing	lifted	retell
immeasurable	faster	misspell	nonfattening
disruption	reflexes	inspector	unlikely

2. Read the following words out loud.

faster	fastest	ticking	slowly	listed	grabbed
flipped	helpful	bags	boxes	helpless	lips

3. Read the following words out loud.

regrettable	permission	incredulous	suppressed
indentured	popular	creativity	philosophical
illegal	accessible	objectify	visionary

[5] The idea for this informal test is credited to Bruce Rosow of the Greenwood School.

LETRS Survey of Morphological Knowledge

Scoring Sheet

1. **Identifying morphemes.** Say, "Read the following words, and circle the prefixes, underline the roots or base words, and box the suffixes. Some words may have no prefix or suffix, or more than one suffix. Watch me do this example."

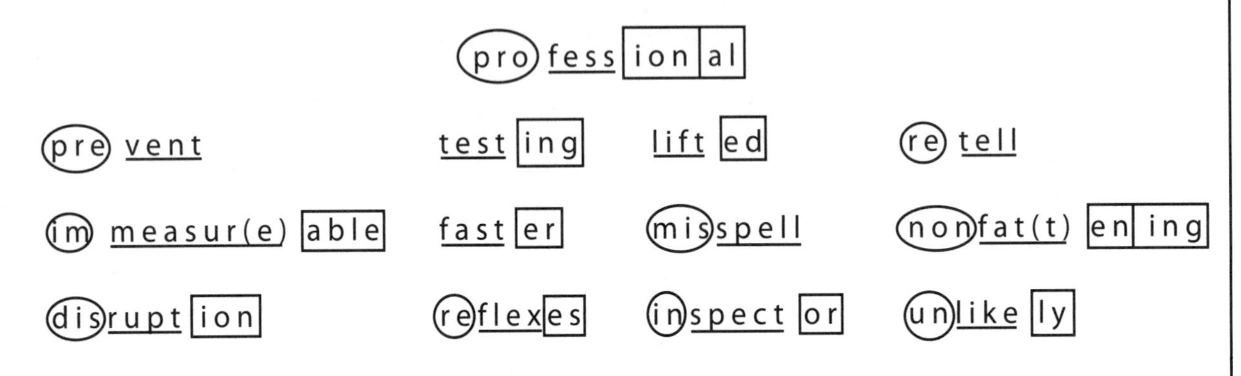

2. **Inflections and common suffixes.** Say, "Read the following words out loud."

faster	fastest	ticking	slowly	listed	grabbed
flipped	helpful	bags	boxes	helpless	lips

3. **Morphologically complex words.** Say, "Read the following words out loud."

regrettable	permission	incredulous	suppressed
indentured	popular	creativity	philosophical
illegal	accessible	objectify	visionary

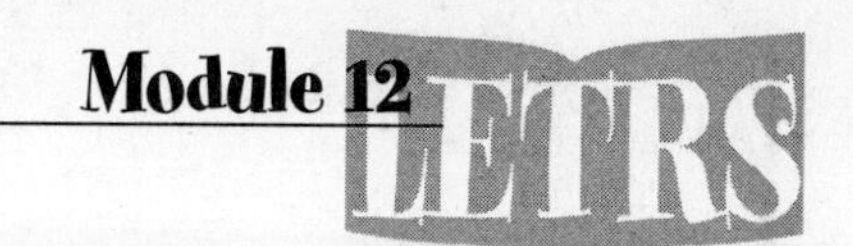

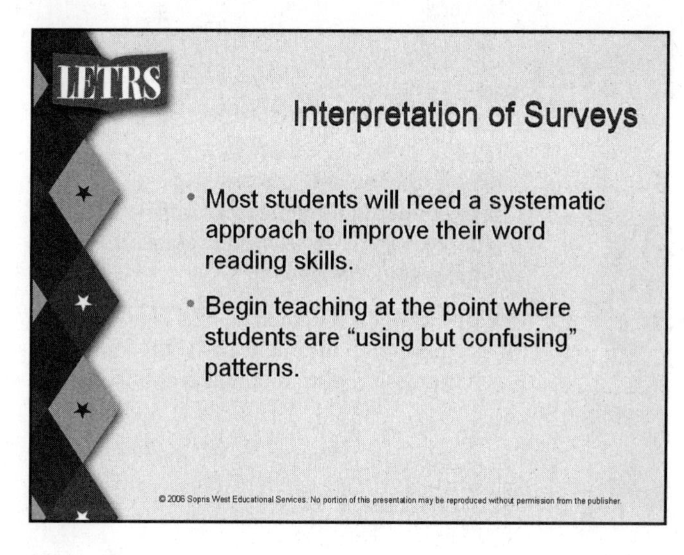

Slide 66

Interpretation of the LETRS Diagnostic Surveys

Most students with reading problems in grade 3 and beyond will benefit from a systematic, sequential, cumulative, explicit approach to word study and phonic decoding. The goal of instruction is to improve accuracy and automaticity of word recognition. Raising of "word consciousness"—that is, understanding of word structure and the correspondence between speech and print—along with lots of practice in guided oral and silent reading of text at the right level of difficulty is the best way to accomplish that goal.

Both of the LETRS surveys should help teachers decide whether instruction needs to begin with single-syllable words or whether multisyllable words and morphemes are the more appropriate level of instruction. Students' knowledge of correspondences for reading can be compared to their knowledge of correspondences for spelling. Any subskills can be explored in greater depth; for example, students' knowledge of the first 300 words on Fry's Instant Words List (Fry, 1999) can be comprehensively surveyed.

LETRS

What About Phonological Skill?

- Reading, spelling, and writing assessments may provide sufficient information to identify phonological processing difficulties.
- Poor spelling, inaccurate and slow word reading, and difficulty with phonics ARE phonological problems.

Slide 67

Assessing Phonological Awareness in Older Students

Research from a variety of sources indicates that phonological processing *tests* for older students do not add power to the identification or prediction of reading and spelling difficulties in this population (Hogan, Catts, & Little, in press). If students have trouble with spelling, phonics, and decoding of nonsense words, they are by definition demonstrating a phonologically-based problem. Tests of phonological processing, such as the Lindamood Auditory Conceptualization Test (LAC) and the Comprehensive Test of Phonological Processing (CTOPP), may verify and highlight phonological problems that are the most common cause of reading and spelling difficulty. Direct measurement of relevant academic skills will provide the most accurate information on which to plan instruction.

Younger students are a different story. Those who have not yet learned to read can be screened with phonemic awareness activities, such as sound segmentation and sound blending, and students who are at risk for reading and spelling problems can be identified. Intervention that includes a strong phonological awareness component can prepare them for reading.

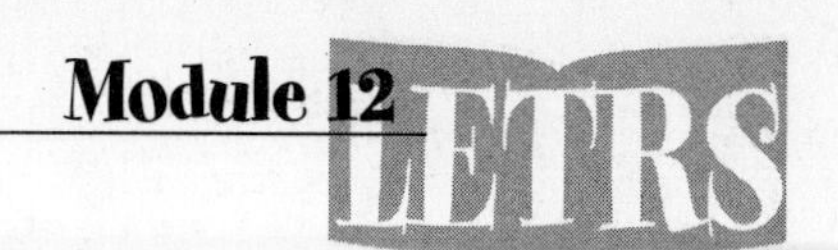

LETRS

Teach Phonologically

- Pronounce words clearly.
- Use key words for sounds.
- Separate, pronounce, and describe speech sounds during spelling and decoding instruction.
- Call attention to articulatory features of sounds.
- Use charts of speech-print correspondences.
- Teach syllable awareness.

Slide 68

However, what we should *teach* is not the same as what we should *test*. Poor readers and spellers in grade 3 and up often need direct remediation of phonological skills in the context of a well-designed reading, spelling, vocabulary, or writing lesson. What does that statement mean? Activities and teaching routines integrated into well-designed lessons include:

- Asking students to recognize if words have been pronounced correctly.
- Asking students to say vocabulary words out loud and to pronounce them correctly.
- Highlighting, describing, and pronouncing individual speech sounds to discriminate similar-sounding words (e.g., **flush**, **flesh**, **fresh**; **entomologist/etymologist**).
- Using a key word or gesture to remind students of a sound's identity.
- Segmenting speech sounds before spelling simple words or to correct misspellings.
- Orally rehearsing the repetition of phrases and sentences that are being written.
- Breaking longer words into syllables orally before spelling those syllables.

LETRS

Exercise #8: Phonological Tasks for Students Beyond Grade 3

- Tools used in research on older, poor readers:
  - **Pig Latin**
  - **Tongue twisters**
  - **Word repetition**
  - **Spoonerisms**

Slide 69

Exercise #8: Phonological Tasks for Students Beyond Grade 3

(For supplementary observation of phonological challenges common in individuals with reading, spelling, and writing difficulty.)

A. **Pig Latin.** Speak a phrase in pig Latin. Remove the first sound from each word in a sentence, put it at the end of the word, and add the sound of the letters **ay** to the end of the word.

Example: Red roses smell sweet.
ed-ray oses-ray mell-say weet-say

B. **Tongue twisters.** Repeat each phrase three times:

Methodist Episcopal
wash each dish twice
shiny seashell necklace
big black bugs' blood
he skied down the snow slope

C. **Word repetition.** Repeat each word one time:

nuclear
animation
philosophical
stethoscope
dyslexic
specifically
syllabication

D. **Spoonerisms** (phonetic "swapping" of initial consonants, word parts, or words themselves). Make a new phrase by switching the initial sounds of the key words.

lead of spite (speed of light)
a well-boiled icicle (a well-oiled bicycle)
tons of soil (sons of toil)
you've tasted two worms (you've wasted two terms)
a half-warmed fish (a half-formed wish)
know your blows (blow your nose)

Table 12.5. Some Assessments Commonly Used for Students Beyond Grade 3

Passage-Reading Comprehension	
Gray Oral Reading Test IV (GORT-IV), Passage Comprehension (Pro-Ed)	Gates-McGinitie Reading Tests
Informal Reading Inventory	Gray Diagnostic Reading Test, Comprehension
Qualitative Reading Inventory	Degrees of Reading Power (DRP)
Passage-Reading Fluency (one-minute timed readings at instructional level)	
DIBELS Intermediate	Reading Fluency Monitor (Read Naturally)
AIMSweb®	
Vocabulary Knowledge (oral language)	
Peabody Picture Vocabulary Test (PPVT)	Wechsler WISC-III or WAIS-III Vocabulary subtests
Test of Word Knowledge (TOWK)	
Word-Recognition Speed and Accuracy	
Test of Word Reading Efficiency (TOWRE)	High-frequency word lists (e.g., Dolch lists)
Test of Silent Word Reading Fluency (TOSWRF)	
Knowledge of Phoneme-Grapheme, Syllable, and Morpheme Correspondences in Orthography	
Timed alphabet writing	Phonics survey:
Developmental spelling inventory (e.g., as found in *Words Their Way*, *Word Journeys*, *LANGUAGE!®*, *Spellography*)	LETRS Phonics and Syllabication Survey
Test of Written Spelling (TWS-4)	LETRS Survey of Morphological Knowledge
Kaufman Test of Educational Achievement, Spelling subtest	Gates-McGinitie Reading Tests (Riverside), Decoding Skills Test
	CORE Phonics Survey
	Shefelbine Phonics Survey
	Word Identification and Spelling Test (WIST) (Pro-Ed)
	Nonsense Word Reading (TOWRE, Woodcock-Johnson)
Phonological Processing	
Comprehensive Test of Phonological Processing (CTOPP)	Analysis of spelling errors (misrepresentation of phonemes and phoneme sequences)
Lindamood Auditory Conceptualization Test (LAC)	Word-repetition tasks
Writing Sample	
Richness of content and ideas; sentence and paragraph structure; discourse organization; choice of words; use of punctuation, capitalization, spelling, and standard English grammar.	

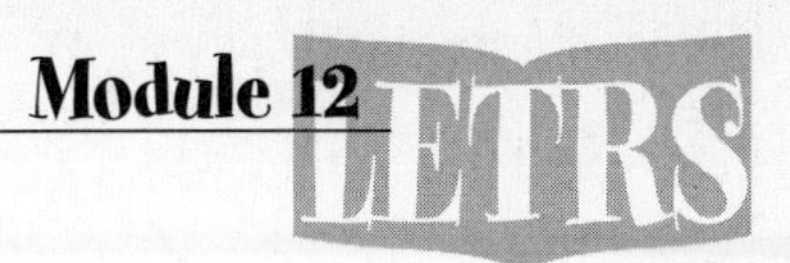

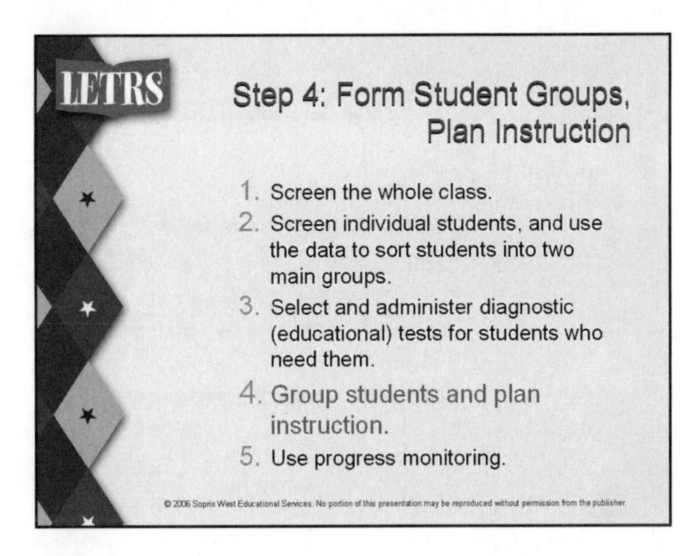

Slide 70

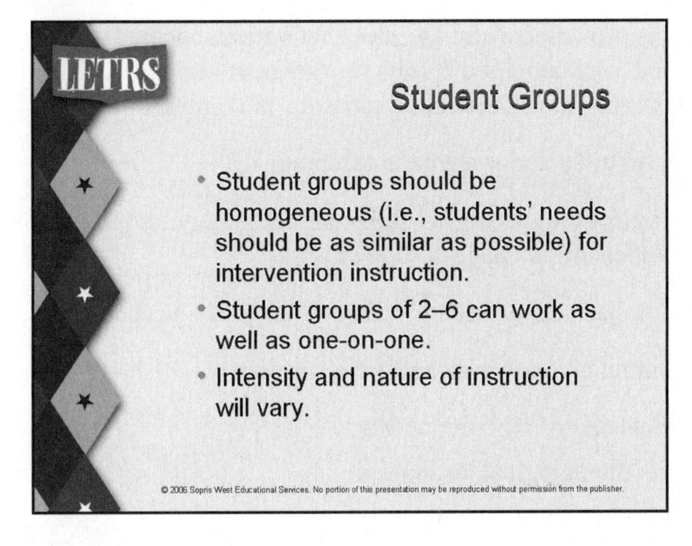

Slide 71

Step 4: Form Student Groups, Plan Instruction

Small groups can range from two to six students. Research suggests that only the most seriously impaired students will need a one-to-one tutorial; even students who need daily remedial instruction can learn as much in small groups of two or three well-matched students as those who receive individual instruction (Vaughn & Linan-Thompson, 2003). Groups designed for intervention, however, must be composed of students with similar instructional needs. One of the reasons why the "resource room" model of special education services has been largely ineffective is that one teacher or program is expected to meet the needs of diverse students. In such situations, the needs of diverse students are unlikely to be satisfactorily met because instruction is not intensive enough to make a difference in an individual student's overall level of achievement.

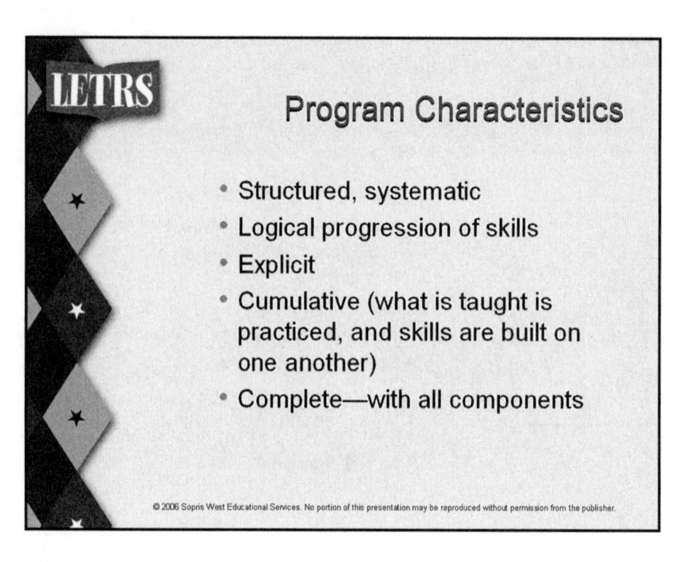

Slide 72

Research is also supporting the idea that various methods and programs can be used to obtain good results (Torgesen et al., 2003). Effective programs, however, have these characteristics in common:

- Structured and systematic teaching.
- Logical progression of skills, based on good developmental models of language-skill acquisition.
- Emphasis on explicit teaching of language structure.
- Cumulative learning and frequent review.
- Inclusion of all components:
    - phonological awareness
    - phonics and word study
    - fluency-building exercises
    - vocabulary development
    - language and reading comprehension
    - spelling and writing
    - ample practice with reading itself.

We recommend that once the assessment results are in hand, teams of grade-level teachers work together in a planning session to decide where each student falls on the continuum of reading development and instructional needs. Use self-stick notes on a big chart that looks like this:

	Spelling and Production of Written Language	PA, Phonics, and Decoding Skill	Fluency	Vocabulary and Reading Comprehension
Strong, established				
Mild weaknesses				
Serious weaknesses				

Even if students share similar testing profiles, their instructional needs may not be exactly alike. Groupings should honor students' personalities, attention capacities, prior history of instruction, general intellectual abilities and interests, and patterns of response to instruction.

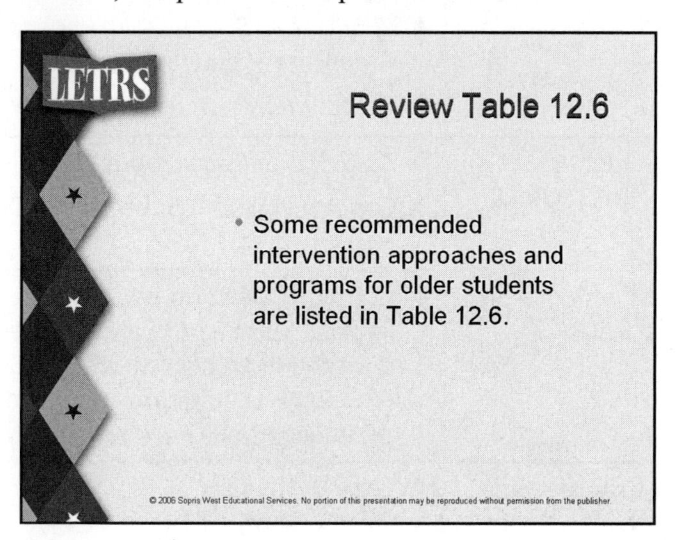

Slide 73

Table 12.6 lists some recommended approaches and programs of instruction for older students that can be used to meet specific student needs. Many of these approaches and programs require professional development to implement effectively.

Table 12.6. Some Recommended Intervention Approaches and Programs for Struggling Readers

Specific Skill Weakness	Typical Tasks That Identify Skill Weaknesses	Remedial Techniques and Approaches
Phoneme identification and manipulation	◆ Remembering, producing, segmenting, and repeating phonemes in spoken words	◆ *Spellography* (Sopris West: 800-547-6747) ◆ *Sounds and Letters for Reading and Spelling* (Sopris West) ◆ *Phonics and Spelling With Phoneme-Grapheme Mapping* (Sopris West) ◆ SIPPS™ (*Systematic Instruction in Phoneme Awareness, Phonics, and Sight Words*): www.devstu.org/sipps
Phoneme-grapheme correspondence, phonics, and syllabication	◆ Giving sounds for single graphemes ◆ Phonics inventory—pattern-based words ◆ Nonsense-word reading	◆ *Sonday System*: www.sondaysystem.com ◆ *Concept Phonics*™: www.oxtonhouse.com ◆ *SpellRead P.A.T.*: www.spellread.com ◆ *Phonics and Spelling With Phoneme-Grapheme Mapping* (Sopris West) ◆ *Spellography* (Sopris West)
Automatic recognition of words by sight	◆ Timed reading of high-frequency words in lists (TOWRE; TOSWR)	◆ *Basic Skill Builders* (Sopris West) ◆ *Concept Phonics*™ Speed Drills (Oxton House)
Speed of naming and word retrieval	◆ Rapid automatic naming of numbers, letters (RAN)	◆ Combine speed drills on sounds, word families, sight words, and phrases with enriched instruction in word meanings (The RAVE-O Program: ase.tufts.edu/crlr/raveo.html)
Alphabet knowledge	◆ Timed alphabet writing ◆ Alphabetizing words	◆ Letter formation ◆ Daily alphabet writing ◆ Alphabetizing practice
Spelling, syllable patterns, and morphology	◆ Dictated, graded word lists with patterned and irregular words; developmental spelling inventory	◆ *Spellography* (Sopris West) ◆ *Sonday System*: www.sondaysystem.com ◆ *SpellRead P.A.T.*: www.spellread.com ◆ *Unlocking Literacy* (Paul H. Brookes Publishing)

Component of Reading	Typical Tests or Indicators	Remedial Programs
Passage fluency	◆ DIBELS Intermediate ◆ Informal Reading Inventory (IRI) ◆ Progress Monitor (in *Read Naturally*)	◆ *Six-Minute Solution* (Sopris West) ◆ *Read Naturally* (800-788-4085): www.readnaturally.com ◆ *Great Leaps*: www.greatleaps.com
Vocabulary	◆ Silent-reading vocabulary test (untimed) (e.g., Gates-McGinitie or IRI) ◆ Peabody Picture Vocab.-III ◆ WISC-III or WAIS Vocab.	◆ (Vocabulary taught with text reading) ◆ *Vocabulary Through Morphology* (Sopris West)
Text comprehension	◆ Degrees of Reading Power (DRP) ◆ Silent passage reading on IRI or Gates-McGinitie ◆ Oral-passage reading with retelling, filling in words (MAZE), answering questions, or DIBELS Retelling Fluency	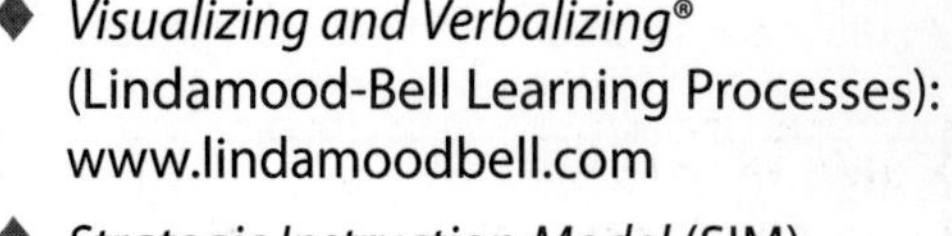 ◆ *Visualizing and Verbalizing*® (Lindamood-Bell Learning Processes): www.lindamoodbell.com ◆ *Strategic Instruction Model* (SIM). University of Kansas: 785-864-4780, www.ku-crl.org ◆ *Reasoning and Reading* (Educators Publishing Service): 800-225-5750 ◆ *Collaborative Strategic Reading* (Sopris West) ◆ *Peer Mediated Learning Strategies* (Sopris West) ◆ Project CRISS (406-758-6440), www.projectcriss.com ◆ *REWARDS Plus, Science and Social Studies* (Sopris West) ◆ Sedita Learning Strategies: www.seditalearning.com

"Are we thinking here, or is this just so much pointing and clicking?"

Technology-Based Reading Programs		
Accelerated Reader®	Monitors student progress in classroom literature.	Renaissance Learning® (866-846-7323)
Scholastic Reading Inventory™—Reading Counts	Easy-to-use, computerized quizzes on high-quality books	Scholastic (800-724-6527): www.scholastic.com
DRP BookLink®	Matches students to books on topics of interest	www.tasaliteracy.com/drpbooklink.htm
Lexile - Pathfinder	Assesses reading levels of students and the difficulty level of texts	www.lexile.com
Lexia Reading SOS	Strategies for older students	(800-435-3942): www.lexialearning.com
READ 180®	Instruction, management, assessment (all integrated)	Scholastic: http://teacher.scholastic.com/products/read180
Start-to-Finish® Books	High-interest fiction for adolescents	Don Johnston (800-999-4660): www.donjohnston.com

Comprehensive Programs for Students With Serious Reading Difficulties	
Corrective Reading series	(grade 4 and up) SRA (800-662-5958)
LANGUAGE!®	(grade 4 and up) Sopris West (800-547-6747)
Wilson Reading System®	Wilson Language (508-869-5699)
LiPS®; *Visualizing and Verbalizing*®; *Seeing Stars*®	Lindamood-Bell (800-233-1819)
Girls and Boys Town Reading Program	Mary Beth Curtis and Anne Marie Longo (402-498-1075): curtism@boystown.org
High Point (approved for ELLs in California)	(800-333-3510): www.hampton-brown.com

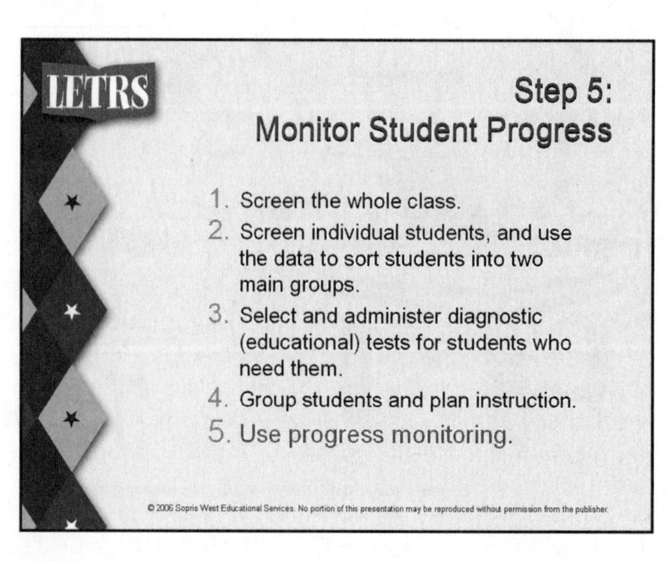

Slide 74

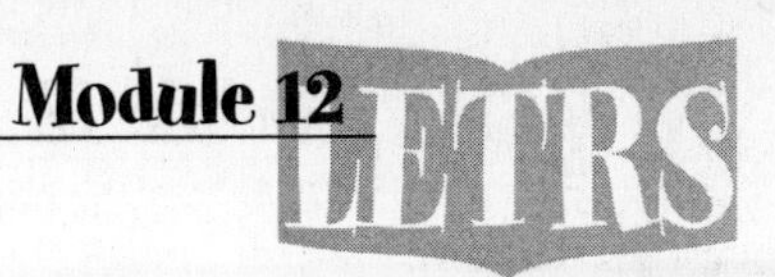

Step 5: Monitor Student Progress

The target skill to monitor with classroom assessments is oral reading fluency with a retelling component because it is such a reliable indicator of overall reading proficiency. Guidelines vary with regard to methods for monitoring individual student progress in oral reading. In their review of curriculum-based measurement research, Hosp and Hosp (2003) advise that teachers need a set of about 30 equivalent passages if they are going to monitor student progress week to week. Many teachers elect to monitor somewhat less often because testing takes time away from instruction. However, if students are more than one grade level behind, their progress should be monitored at least every three to four weeks.

A promising new tool for monitoring student progress in both essential reading skills and text reading comprehension is the MASI: Multilevel Academic Skills Inventory-Reading (Hosp et al., in development). The MASI is a set of curriculum-based materials and evaluation procedures designed for use in diagnosing reading problems and monitoring response to instruction. Because most of the measures are timed, the critical factor of fluency is taken into account in determining student growth. Originally developed by Kenneth Howell, MASI is being revised and piloted by Michelle and John Hosp.

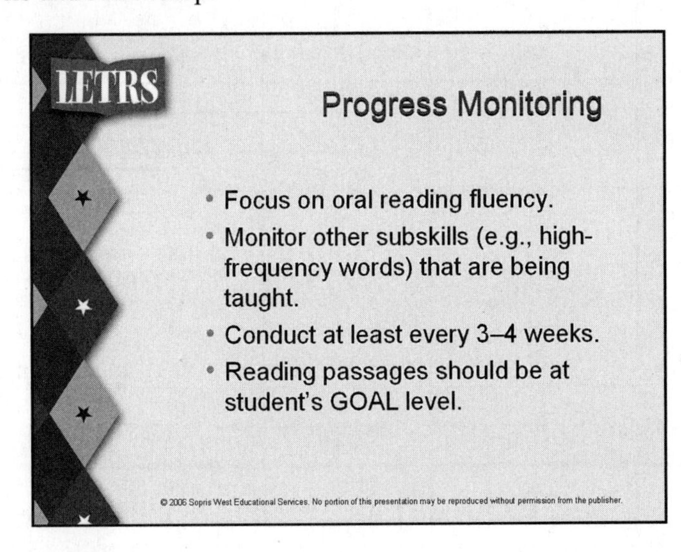

Slide 75

At grades 1 and 2, progress monitoring passages should be at the student's instructional level. At grade 3 and above, however, passages should be at the student's **goal** level—that is, the level of oral reading fluency that is considered to be: (a) about a grade level higher than the student is currently functioning; or (b) a level expected for that student's age and/or grade. Progress should be compared to an "aim line," or trajectory, of expected growth toward a goal.

Normative expectations for growth in reading fluency are well established. Hasbrouck and Tindal (1992) collected and published norms

in 1992, which have recently been revised on the basis of a very large sample (Hasbrouck & Tindal, 2005). Those norms are listed below.

Table 12.7. Oral Reading Fluency Norms—Grades 1–8 (Hasbrouck & Tindal, 2005)

Compiled by Jan Hasbrouck, Ph.D., and Gerald Tindal, Ph.D.

GRADE	PERCENTILE	FALL WCPM	WINTER WCPM	SPRING WCPM
1	90		81	111
	75		47	82
	50		23	53
	25		12	28
	10		6	15
	SD		32	39
	Count		16950	19434
2	90	106	125	142
	75	79	100	117
	50	51	72	89
	25	25	42	61
	10	11	18	31
	SD	37	41	42
	Count	15896	18229	20128
3	90	128	146	162
	75	99	120	137
	50	71	92	107
	25	44	62	78
	10	21	36	48
	SD	40	43	44
	Count	16988	17383	18372
4	90	145	166	180
	75	119	139	152
	50	94	112	123
	25	68	87	98
	10	45	61	72
	SD	40	41	43
	Count	16523	14572	16269

WCPM = Words correct per minute

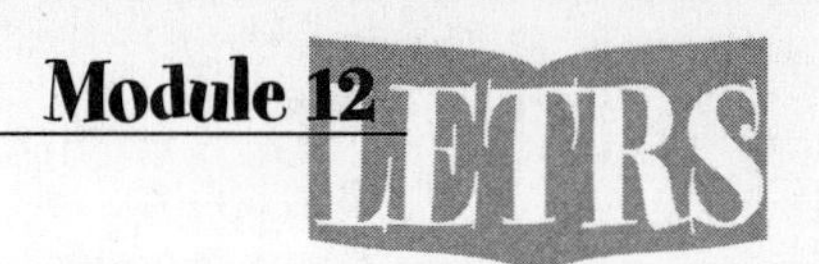

GRADE	PERCENTILE	FALL WCPM	WINTER WCPM	SPRING WCPM
5	90	166	182	194
	75	139	156	168
	50	110	127	139
	25	85	99	109
	10	61	74	83
	SD	45	44	45
	Count	16212	13331	15292
6	90	177	195	204
	75	153	167	177
	50	127	140	150
	25	98	111	122
	10	68	82	93
	SD	42	45	44
	Count	10520	9218	11290
7	90	180	192	202
	75	156	165	177
	50	128	136	150
	25	102	109	123
	10	79	88	98
	SD	40	43	41
	Count	6482	4058	5998
8	90	185	199	199
	75	161	173	177
	50	133	146	151
	25	106	115	124
	10	77	84	97
	SD	43	45	41
	Count	5546	3496	5335

WCPM = Words correct per minute

Used with permission of Jan Hasbrouck and Gerry Tindal.

Table summarized from Behavioral Research & Teaching (2005, January). *Oral Reading Fluency: 90 Years of Measurement* (BRT Technical Report No. 33). Eugene: University of Oregon, College of Education.

Data available at: http://brt.uoregon.edu/Publications and Materials/ Technical Reports.

Table available at: www.jhasbrouck.com/ORF2005_dataBRT.pdf.

LETRS

Chart Progress Monitoring Results

Fifth Grade Scoring Booklet

Slide 76

DIBELS®
6th Edition

Name: ______________________

Teacher: ______________________

140 120 100 80 60 40 20

Sept. Scores | Oct. Scores | Nov. Scores | Dec. Scores | Jan. Scores | Feb. Scores | March Scores | April Scores | May Scores | June Scores

Wk 1 ____
Wk 2 ____
Wk 3 ____
Wk 4 ____

*Each tick is 4 points.

Fifth Grade Scoring Booklet
Progress Monitoring
Oral Reading Fluency

Progress Monitoring Probe 13

Kerri Strug

When she was nineteen, Kerri Strug became known	8
worldwide as the brave young woman who competed in the	18
Olympics and helped her team in the overall gymnastics	27
competition. During that competition, her team won the gold	36
medal.	37
Kerri was born in Arizona and was very active as a child.	49
When she was young, she liked to walk through the house on her	62
hands. She also sometimes sped through the house on her	72
tricycle. At one point, her home had a large carpeted room with	84
no furniture. Kerri used the room as her private gym, doing	95
cartwheels, handstands, and flips. She was very disappointed	103
when her parents moved furniture into it.	110
When Kerri was older, she had to make a difficult decision.	121
She realized that she had the skills as a gymnast to make it to the	136
Olympics. She also realized that to reach this goal, she would	147
need to be taught by the best coach she could find. She found a	161
skilled coach in Texas and decided to move there. Even though	172
she lived with different friends, she was sometimes lonely while	182
she was there. She called her parents often for support. Her	193
parents were very proud of her and excited to talk to her about	206
her work and life as a gymnast.	213
Her coach had Kerri practice eight hours a day, six or seven	225
days a week. He also required her to stay on a strict training	238
schedule and to go to bed at a certain hour. Luckily, her aunt and	252
uncle lived nearby. When she occasionally went to visit them,	262
she would enjoy a more relaxed schedule than during her	272
training. She even got to stay up past her bedtime to watch	284
television.	285

Kerri Strug (Continued)

After her experiences at the Olympics, Kerri worked to help	295
children learn how to overcome difficulties to reach their goals.	305
She gave talks about the dangers of drugs and alcohol and helped	317
raise money for the Make-A-Wish Foundation and Special	327
Olympics. Kerri has written two books. One book, *Landing on*	337
My Feet, a Diary of Dreams, tells about her life up until the	350
Olympic games. *Heart of Gold* gives encouragement and advice	359
for children to use to reach their own dreams.	368

Retell: ORF Total:________

⊗ • • • • • • • • • • * • • • • • • • • • • * • • • • • • • • • • *	30
⊗ • • • • • • • • • • * • • • • • • • • • • * • • • • • • • • • • *	60
⊗ • • • • • • • • • • * • • • • • • • • • • * • • • • • • • • • • *	90
⊗ • • • • • • • • • • * • • • • • • • • • • * • • • • • • • • • • *	120
⊗ • • • • • • • • • • * • • • • • • • • • • * • • • • • • • • • • *	150
⊗ • • • • • • • • • • * • • • • • • • • • • * • • • • • • • • • • *	180

Retell Total:________

Notes:

Instructional Problem Solving Through Case Study Analyses

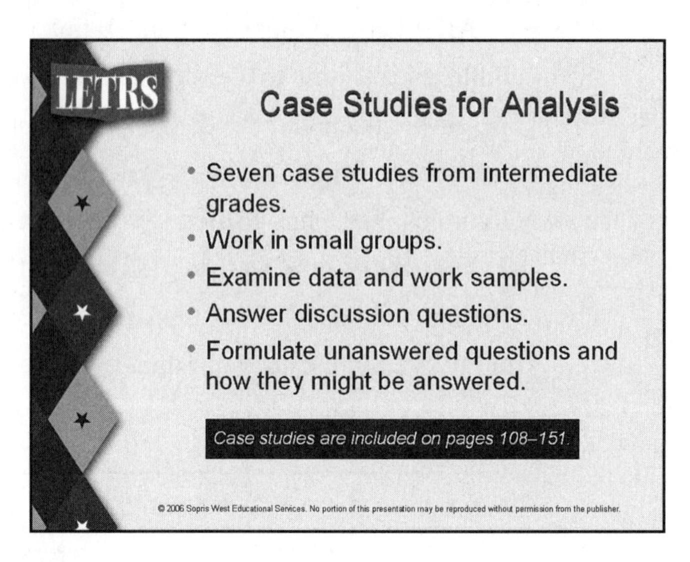

Slide 77

Introduction to Case Studies

The following case study participants are intermediate students in a school that has received a Reading First grant. The student-study personnel—including reading teachers, special education teachers, the principal, an ESL teacher, a school psychologist, and classroom teachers (when appropriate)—carry out the individual testing and confer weekly about the students receiving intervention instruction. Faculty members understand that students in the "strategic" range on DIBELS need less intensive instruction than students who score in the "intensive" range. All of the support staff is trained to deliver one or more systematic structured language programs that are taught to groups of two–six students, four days per week. Students are grouped for instruction within their classrooms as well. In addition to whole-group instruction, each classroom teacher instructs three small groups each day for 20–30 minutes.

The assessment process is similar to what is outlined in this module. First, students are screened with the silent passage reading placement test that is included with the core comprehensive reading program. In addition, students take the six-week unit tests of the core comprehensive program, which include silent passage reading with multiple-choice questions. Silent word reading fluency is not yet included in the school's assessment program.

Next, those students who score below 75% correct on the reading program's placement test or on a unit test are given an individually administered oral reading test for fluency and comprehension. In this school, both the Informal Reading Inventory that is included with the core comprehensive program and the Gray Oral Reading Tests, Fourth Edition (GORT-4), are used. The Peabody Picture Vocabulary Test-Third Edition (PPVT-III) is given to assess vocabulary knowledge, as it does not require reading skill. Every teacher conducts a developmental spelling inventory with his or her own class.

Third, those students who score below grade-level criterion in oral reading fluency (about the 40th percentile) are given additional assessments. These assessments vary and are chosen by the student-study team on the basis of the student's apparent strengths and weaknesses. Typically, students will complete an informal inventory of phoneme awareness and phonics skill, as well as the Test of Word Reading Efficiency (TOWRE), to ascertain where their instruction needs to begin.

Fourth, the student-study team collaborates to determine the intensity, content, type, and predicted duration of instruction for each student who is not at grade level. Finally, progress monitoring assessments are employed every few weeks to determine how well students are responding to their instructional program. Only students who are not responding well to intervention or students with known handicapping conditions are referred for special education evaluations. School resources and teacher time are devoted to instruction as much as possible. Weekly team meetings of all support personnel are used to examine students' test data, including progress monitoring, and to reconsider instructional groupings and programs.

The following case studies are presented for analysis and small-group discussion. They represent the spectrum of problems that are typical of students who are not proficient in reading, spelling, oral language, and/or written composition.

Case Study #1: Aaron, Grade 4 (assessed in September)

SKILL ASSESSED	ASSESSMENT TOOL(S)	RESULTS
Silent passage reading with multiple-choice questions, time-limited: **Vocabulary** **Comprehension**	Reading program Placement test	36% correct on silent reading vocabulary. Comprehension at beginning fourth grade-level passage.
Silent word recognition, timed.	(Not given)	
Oral passage reading fluency and accuracy.	Informal reading inventory	93% accuracy on third-grade level.
	Gray Oral Reading Test IV (GORT-IV)	25th percentile on accuracy. 25th percentile on rate. Overall fluency, 16th percentile (standard score 85).
Oral passage reading comprehension.	Gray Oral Reading Test IV (GORT-IV)	25th percentile
Oral word reading efficiency: **Real words** **Nonsense words**	Test of Word Reading Efficiency (TOWRE)	Real word list: 2.8 grade equivalent. Nonsense word list: 1.8 grade equivalent (fast, but inaccurate at decoding).
Phonological awareness screen: **Rhyme production** **Syllable counting** **Phoneme segmentation** **Phoneme manipulation and conceptualization**	Informal screening	Errors on syllable counting, phoneme segmentation, and identification of words in sentences.
Vocabulary development.	Peabody Picture Vocabulary Test-Third Edition (PPVT-III)	23rd percentile
Inventory of decoding skills: **Areas of strength** **Areas of need**	(TOWRE error analysis)	Multiple errors on: simple closed syllables blends and digraphs in closed syllables VC**e** Vowel-**r** combinations
Developmental spelling inventory: **Number correct** **Areas of need**	(Not available)	

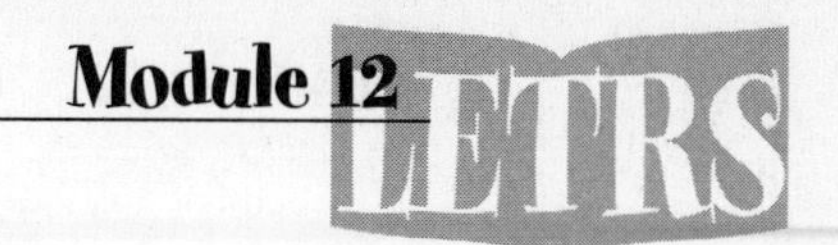

Writing Sample

CASE STUDY #1

The best theing in school is math you can
ren a lot of your moitneshand your adlmoitnes
and srtat you can do lots of suft in Math
like round the oneor ten you can do it to you can
wen nede you can do both to gith.

CASE STUDY #1 - Spelling Inventory

1. shel — 15. chakh
2. theing — 16. phon
3. crabp — 17. sash
4. clek — 18. puont
5. chek — 19. surte
6. bksh — 20. drleg
7. brka — 21. prapf
8. dlad — 22. wefg
9. ftrt — 23. powrfl
10. kwaf — 24. betta

CASE STUDY #1 - "Aaron" (Errors are circled.)

Spellography Spelling Inventory — Individual Score Sheet

Name

Date 8-15-03

Features	Short Vowel	Digrph Trigrph	Blend	VCE	Complex Cons.	Vowel + R	Vowel Teams	Inflections	Syllable juncture	Prefix	Final Syllable/ Suffix	Root morph	Extra Point/ correct	Point Totals
1. shell	e	sh			**ll**									2
2. thing	i	th/ng												3
3. cramp	a		cr**mp**											2
4. slick	**i**	**ck**	**sl**											0
5. chunk	**u**	**ch**	**nk**											0
6. blotch	**o**	**tch**	bl											1
7. broke			br	**o-e**										1
8. glade			**gl**	**a-e**										0
9. fright			fr				**igh**							1
10. quite			**qu**	**i-e**										0
11. dream			dr				**ea**							1
12. throat			thr				**oa**							1
13. nurse					**-se**	**ur**								0
14. scrape			**scr**	**a-e**										0
15. charge		ch			**-ge**	**ar**								1
16. phone		ph		**o-e**										1
17. smudge	**u**		**sm**		**-dge**									0
18. point			nt				**oi**							1
19. squirt			**squ**			**ir**								0
20. drawing			dr				**aw**	**-ing**						1
21. trapped			**tr**					**-ed**	**pp**					0
22. waving								**-ing**	**v (e)**					0
23. powerful						**er**	ow				**-ful**			1
24. battle									tt		**-tle**			1
25. refused								**-ed**		**re**		**fus**		0
26. lesson									**ss**		**-on**			0
27. pennies								**-ies**	**nn**					0
28. fraction											**-tion**	**frac**		0
29. sailor											**-or**	**sail**		0
30. distance											**-ance**	**dist**		0
31. conduction										**con**	**-tion**	**duc**		0
32. discovery											**-ery**	**cov**		0
33. resident										**re**	**-ent**	**sid(e)**		0
34. visible											**-ible**	**vis**		0
#/Color Code	3/[illegible]	5/8	8/17	0/5	0/4	0/4	1/6	0/[illegible]	1/6	0/[illegible]	0/10	0/[illegible]	0/[illegible]	18/114

Feature totals in bottom row are colored in as follows: Red = 2+ errors; Yellow = 1 error; Green = 0 errors.

Questions for Discussion and Analysis, Case Study #1

1. What does this student's *instructional* reading level appear to be?
2. About where does this student rank on the normal curve? Are there signs of a discrepancy between the student's overall verbal abilities and his reading fluency and comprehension, or is the student functioning at about the expected level?
3. Does this student need instruction in decoding skill? What is the basis for your opinion?
4. Does this student need help developing better phonological awareness? What is the basis for your opinion?
5. Would this student benefit from exercises designed specifically to enhance reading fluency? On what do you base your opinion?
6. Would you expect this student to comprehend well if his fluency and accuracy in word reading were bolstered? What is the implication of your opinion?
7. What other questions would you like to address with additional diagnostic testing, record review, or interviews before planning instruction with this student?
8. Outline your plan for helping this student.

   A. Intensity of instruction:

   ____

   ____

   ____

   B. Content emphasis (goals) of instruction:

   ____

   ____

   ____

   C. Possible programs, methods, or approaches:

   ____

   ____

   ____

Case Study #2: T.L., Grade 5, age 10-11 (assessed in September)

SKILL ASSESSED	ASSESSMENT TOOL(S)	RESULTS
Silent passage reading with multiple-choice questions, time-limited: **Vocabulary** **Comprehension**	Reading program Placement test Unit Test 1	48% correct on silent reading. Vocabulary and comprehension at beginning fifth grade-level passage. 28% correct on multiple-choice questions.
Silent word recognition, timed.	(Not given)	
Oral passage reading fluency and accuracy.	Informal reading inventory	60 WCPM with 19 errors on fourth-grade level (discontinued, too hard); 70 WCPM on lower passage.
	Gray Oral Reading Test IV (GORT-IV)	Overall fluency: below the 1st percentile.
Oral passage reading comprehension.	Gray Oral Reading Test IV (GORT-IV)	Below the 2nd percentile
Oral word reading efficiency: **Real words** **Nonsense words**	Test of Word Reading Efficiency (TOWRE)	Real word list: 1.6 grade equivalent. Nonsense word list: 1.6 grade equivalent (very slow).
Phonological awareness screen: **Rhyme production** **Syllable counting** **Phoneme segmentation** **Phoneme manipulation and conceptualization**	Informal screening	Strong on all skills except syllable counting.
Vocabulary development.	Peabody Picture Vocabulary Test-Third Edition (PPVT-III)	95th percentile
Inventory of decoding skills: **Areas of strength** **Areas of need**		Decodes sound-by-sound, knows single-consonant and short-vowel correspondences.
Developmental spelling inventory: **Number correct** **Areas of need**	(Spelling error analysis on writing sample)	Doesn't know sounds for these graphemes: **ar**, **-y**, VC**e**, **oo**, **all**, **ck**

GRAY ORAL READING

TL Grade 5
CASE STUDY
#2

Story 2

Prompt: Say, "This story is about an animal. Read the story to find what the animal does."
Maximum words examiner may provide: 8

1 **Our cat Mimi likes to sit on the roof.**
2 **Mimi goes up the tall tree by the house.**
3 **Then she jumps on the roof.**
4 **She sits and looks at birds.**
5 **But she always comes down when it is time to eat.**

Time (in seconds): 91 Deviations from Print: 6

Comprehension Questions

B **1.** The cat in the story sits ____.
A. by the house
B. on top of the house
C. in a tree
D. by the fire

B **2.** The cat in the story ____.
A. likes to see birds
B. eats birds
C. sleeps under the tree
D. cannot get down

C **3.** What does Mimi like best?
A. the tree
B. the grass
C. the roof
D. the bed

B **4.** What does *not* go in the story?
A. There are many things to see from the roof.
B. Mimi has fun on the roof.
C. There is snow on the roof.
D. Sometimes Mimi sleeps on the roof.

B **5.** Why do you think Mimi likes to sit on the roof?
A. It is cool.
B. It is easy to find food.
C. It feels safe.
D. It is a good joke.

2 Comprehension Score

Converting Time and Deviations from Print to Rate and Accuracy

Rate/Accuracy Scores	0	1	2	3	4	5
Time	>119	67–119	52–66	36–51	22–35	<22
Deviations from Print	>11	8–11	6–7	3–5	2	0–1

Rate Score 1 + Accuracy Score 2 = Fluency Score 3

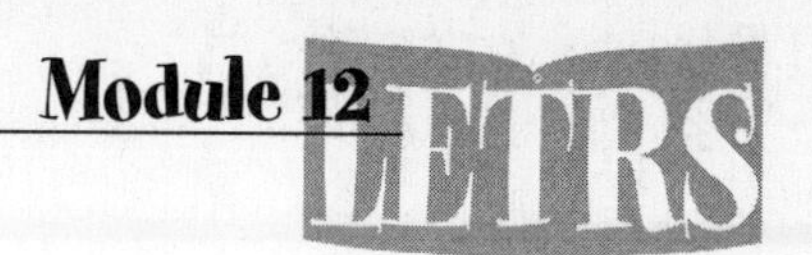

CASE STUDY #2

U

11-17-03
Writing Sample

one day Quinn and I
went to the Student
coulls prade we got
candey and techushts. We
got to see coull cars
and we got to mis going
to the church and we
got to wroch fullball if
we wmttato.

Name T.L. Grade 5 (CASE STUDY #2) Date

♦ Write a story about the first birthday you can remember. Describe what your day was like and how it felt to be one year older.

My Birthday Was gud becuse
I had all mx frends at
mx pote, my frend Chris and
mx frend mick. we eat cack and
ice crem. We plad futboll.
We rod bics

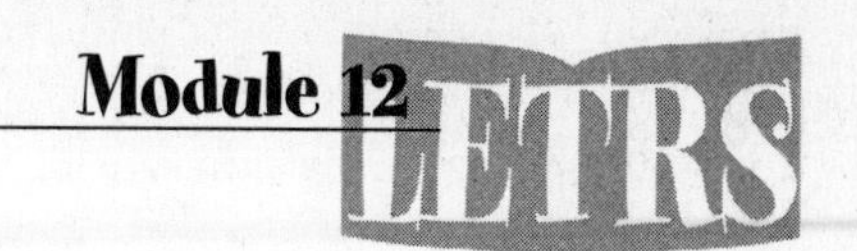

CASE STUDY #2

12-16-03

1. Shell
2. thing
3. cramp
4. Slick
5. chank
6. bloch
7. brok
8. glad
9. frite
10. guite — stated the first letter is "b."
11. dreme
12. throte.
13. nurs
14. Scrape
15. choj

Spellography Spelling Inventory — Individual Score Sheet							Name CASE STUDY # 2				Date 2-16-03			
Features	Short Vowel	Digraph Trigraph	Blend	VCE	Complex Cons.	Vowel + R	Vowel Teams	Inflections	Syllable Juncture	Prefix	Final Syllable/ Suffix	Root Morph	Extra Point/ Correct	Point Totals
1. shell	e	sh			ll								1	4
2. thing	i	th/ng											1	3
3. cramp	a		cr/mp										1	2
4. slick	i	ck	sl										1	3
5. chunk	u	ch	nk										1	3
6. blotch	o	tch	bl											2
7. broke			br	o-e										1
8. glade			gl	a-e										1
9. fright			fr				igh							1
10. quite			qu	i-e										
11. dream			dr				ea							1
12. throat			thr				oa							1
13. nurse					-se	ur								1
14. scrape			scr	a-e										1
15. charge		ch			-ge	ar								1
16. phone		ph		o-e								Total	5/15	25/47
17. smudge	u		sm		-dge									
18. point			nt				oi							
19. squirt			squ			ir								
20. drawing			dr				aw	-ing						
21. trapped			tr					-ed	pp					
22. waving								-ing	-v (e)					
23. powerful						er	ow				-ful			
24. battle									tt		-tle			
25. refused								-ed		re		fus		
26. lesson									ss		-on			
27. pennies								-ies	nn					
28. fraction											-tion	frac		
29. sailor											-or	sail		
30. distance											-ance	dist		
31. conduction										con	-tion	duc		
32. discovery											-ery	cov		
33. resident										re	-ent	sid(e)		
34. visible											-ible	vis		
#/Color Code	/7	/8	/17	/5	/4	/4	/6	/5	/5	/3	/10	/8	/34	/116

Feature totals in bottom row are colored in as follows: Red = 2+ errors; Yellow = 1 error; Green = 0 errors.

Questions for Discussion and Analysis, Case Study #2

1. What does this student's *instructional* reading level appear to be?
2. About where does this student rank on the normal curve? Can you tell if there is a discrepancy between the student's overall verbal abilities and his reading fluency and comprehension?
3. Does this student need instruction in decoding skill? What is the basis for your opinion?
4. Does this student need help developing better phonological awareness? What is the basis for your opinion?
5. Would this student benefit from exercises designed specifically to enhance reading fluency? On what do you base your opinion?
6. Would you expect this student to comprehend well if his fluency and accuracy in word reading were bolstered? What is the implication of your opinion?
7. What other questions would you like to address with additional diagnostic testing, record review, or interviews before planning instruction with this student?
8. Outline your plan for helping this student.

   A. Intensity of instruction:

   B. Content emphasis (goals) of instruction:

   C. Possible programs, methods, or approaches:

Case Study #3: A.C., beginning Grade 4

SKILL ASSESSED	ASSESSMENT TOOL(S)	RESULTS
Silent passage reading with multiple-choice questions, time-limited: **Vocabulary** **Comprehension**	Reading program Placement test	70% accurate total score. 65% correct on vocabulary. 86% correct on comprehension questions.
Silent word recognition, timed.	(Not given)	
Oral passage reading fluency and accuracy.	Informal reading inventory	80 WCPM, 98% accurate on oral reading passage. 80% comprehension accuracy on beginning fourth grade-level passage.
	Gray Oral Reading Test IV (GORT-IV)	(Not given)
Oral passage reading comprehension.	Gray Oral Reading Test IV (GORT-IV)	(Not given)
Oral word reading efficiency: **Real words** **Nonsense words**	Test of Word Reading Efficiency (TOWRE)	(Not given)
Phonological awareness screen: **Rhyme production** **Syllable counting** **Phoneme segmentation** **Phoneme manipulation and conceptualization**	Informal screening	(Not given)
Vocabulary development.	Peabody Picture Vocabulary Test-Third Edition (PPVT-III)	(Not given)
Inventory of decoding skills: **Areas of strength** **Areas of need**		(Not given)
Developmental spelling inventory: **Number correct** **Areas of need**	(Not given)	(Not given)

My favorite Activity in school so far is?

CASE STUDY #3

Nov/14/2005

final copy

My favorit activity school So far is outdoor with hiking night programs and the high school leaders. Although hiking isn't lots of fun it is tiering too I learned alot by Hiking on the forestry traill. Night programs was when the fog man came he Sang song played music He Scared All of the kid in the room it was funny. The High school leaders I only know a few of the leaders I know miss Brenna miss Sinton mr. Z and mr. Jasper they are the coolist High School leaders Even they should teach 6th grade Out door lab was my favorite activity So far this year

CASE 3

Aug 13
Spelli

1. shell
2. Thing
3. cramne cramp
4. slihe slick
5. Ounh chunk
6. Plach blotch
7. Brohe
8. glade
9. fright
10. quite
11. Dream

+6

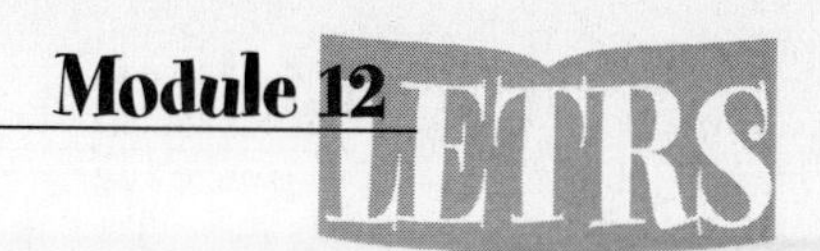

CASE 3

Aug 14 2003
Spelling

12. throught — oa
13. nurse
14. scrape
15. charge
16. phone
17. smuge — dge
18. point
19. squirt
20. Drawing
21. trape — pp ed
22. waving
23. powerful
24. battle
25. refused
26. leasson
27. pennies
28. fraction
29. sailor
30. distance
31. Conduction
32. discovery
33. resident
34. visibls — ible

CASE STUDY #3

Spellography Spelling Inventory — Individual Score Sheet

Features	Short Vowel	Digrph Trigrph	Blend	VCE	Complex Cons.	Vowel + R	Vowel Teams	Inflections	Syllable juncture	Prefix	Final Syllable/ Suffix	Root morph	Extra Point/ correct	Point Totals
1. shell	e	sh			ll								1	
2. thing	i	th/ng											1	
3. cramp	a		~~cr/mp~~											
4. slick	i	~~ck~~	sl											
5. chunk	u	~~ch~~	nk											
6. blotch	~~o~~	~~tch~~	~~bl~~											
7. broke			br	o-e									1	
8. glade			gl	a-e									1	
9. fright			fr				igh						1	
10. quite			qu	~~i-e~~										
11. dream			dr				ea						1	
12. throat			thr				~~oa~~							
13. nurse					-se	ur							1	
14. scrape			scr	a-e									1	
15. charge		ch			-ge	ar							1	
16. phone		ph		o-e									1	
17. smudge	u		sm		~~dge~~									
18. point			nt				oi						1	
19. squirt			squ			ir							1	
20. drawing			dr				aw	-ing					1	
21. trapped			tr					~~-ed~~	~~pp~~					
22. waving								-ing	-v (e)				1	
23. powerful						er	ow				-ful		1	
24. battle									tt		-tle		1	
25. refused								-ed		re		fus	1	
26. lesson									ss		-on			
27. pennies								-ies	nn				1	
28. fraction											-tion	frac	1	
29. sailor											-or	sail	1	
30. distance											-ance	dist	1	
31. conduction										con	-tion	duc	1	
32. discovery											-ery	cov	1	
33. resident										re	-ent	sid(e)	1	
34. visible											~~-ible~~	vis		
#/Color Code	6/7	5/8	14/17	4/5	3/4	4/4	5/6	4/5	4/5	3/3	9/10	8/8	24/34	93/~~125~~ 116

Feature totals in bottom row are colored in as follows: Red = 2+ errors; Yellow = 1 error; Green = 0 errors.

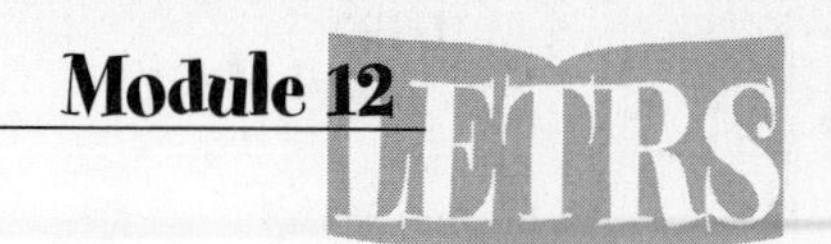

Questions for Discussion and Analysis, Case Study #3

1. What does this student's *instructional* reading level appear to be?
2. About where does this student rank on the normal curve?
3. Does this student need instruction in decoding skill? What is the basis for your opinion?
4. Does this student need help developing better phonological awareness? What is the basis for your opinion?
5. Would this student benefit from exercises designed specifically to enhance reading fluency? On what do you base your opinion?
6. Would you expect this student to comprehend better if her fluency was bolstered? What is the implication of your opinion?
7. Are there other questions you would like to address with additional diagnostic testing, record review, or interviews before planning instruction with this student?
8. What does the writing sample indicate about this student's expressive language and writing abilities?
9. Outline your plan for helping this student.

   A. Intensity of instruction:

   B. Content emphasis (goals) of instruction:

   C. Possible programs, methods, or approaches:

Case Study #4: Cheri, Grade 5 (assessed at beginning of Grade 5)

SKILL ASSESSED	ASSESSMENT TOOL(S)	RESULTS
Silent passage reading with multiple-choice questions, time-limited: **Vocabulary** **Comprehension**	Reading program Placement test	89 % correct on silent reading vocabulary. Comprehension at beginning fifth grade-level passage.
Silent word recognition, timed.	(Not given)	
Oral passage reading fluency and accuracy.	Informal reading inventory	99% accuracy, 142 WCPM on fifth grade-level passage. 100% comprehension correct.
	Gray Oral Reading Test IV (GORT-IV)	(Not given)
Oral passage reading comprehension.	Gray Oral Reading Test IV (GORT-IV)	(Not given)
Oral word reading efficiency: **Real words** **Nonsense words**	Test of Word Reading Efficiency (TOWRE)	(Not given)
Phonological awareness screen: **Rhyme production** **Syllable counting** **Phoneme segmentation** **Phoneme manipulation and conceptualization**	Informal screening	(Not given)
Vocabulary development	Peabody Picture Vocabulary Test-Third Edition (PPVT-III)	(Not given)
Inventory of decoding skills: **Areas of strength** **Areas of need**	(Not given)	(Not given)
Developmental spelling inventory: **Number correct** **Areas of need**	(Not given)	(Not given)

CA
Grade 5

Name CASE STUDY #4 Date

- Write a story about the first birthday you can remember. Describe what your day was like and how it felt to be one year older.

The first birthday I can remember is my 7th birthday. I had my first birthday party. I had so much fun! My sister came and all my friends. We had a great cake that had a picture of four girls one jumproper, a cheerleader a gymnist, and a dancer. We had a lot of prizes for the people who won games. When I blew out the candles and turned 7 years old I felt like I could do more things and I was going to be in 2nd grade. That is first birth-day I can remember.

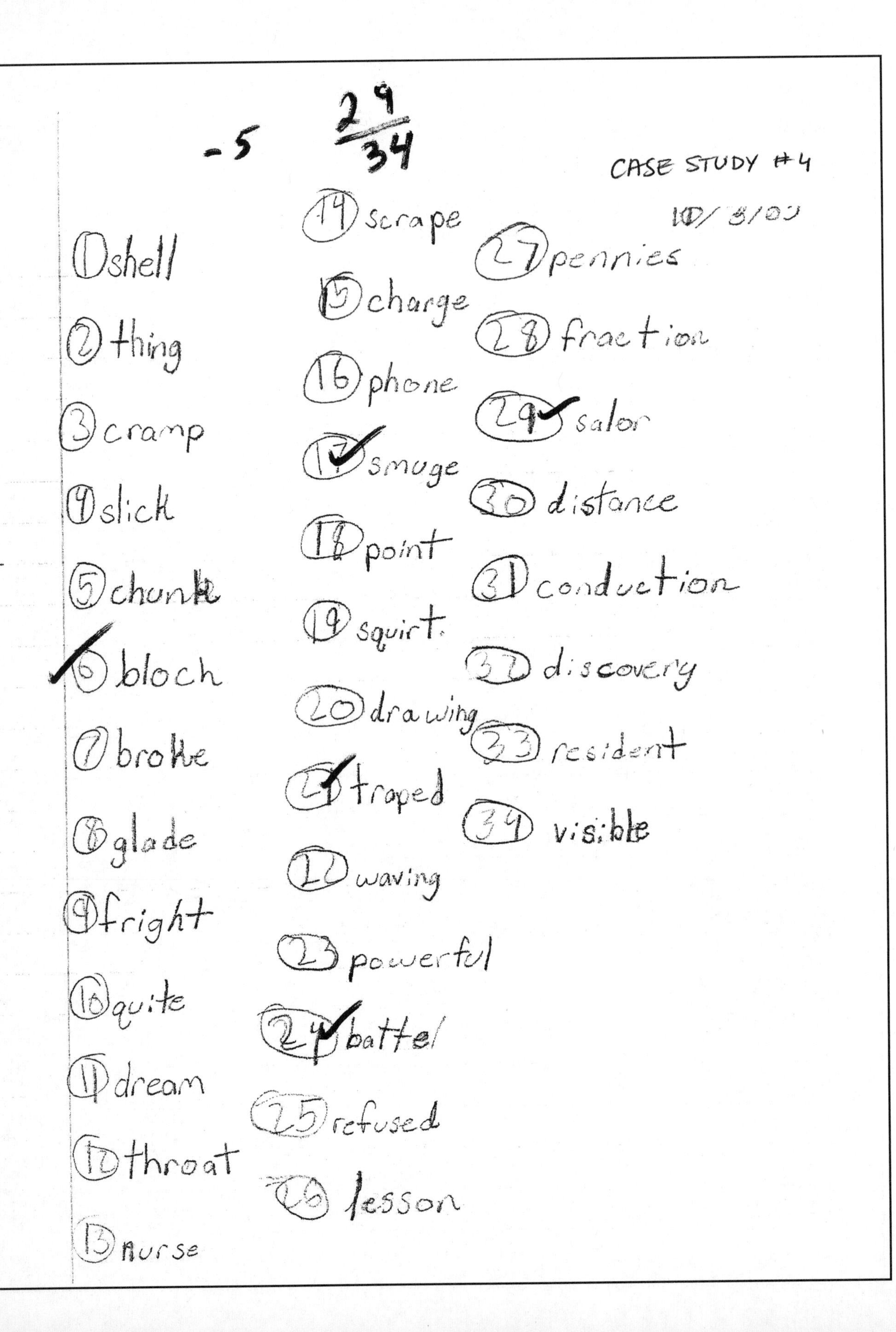
-5
29/34
CASE STUDY #4
10/3/03
1 shell
2 thing
3 cramp
4 slick
5 chunk
6 bloch
7 broke
8 glade
9 fright
10 quite
11 dream
12 throat
13 nurse
14 scrape
15 charge
16 phone
17 smuge
18 point
19 squirt
20 drawing
21 traped
22 waving
23 powerful
24 battel
25 refused
26 lesson
27 pennies
28 fraction
29 salor
30 distance
31 conduction
32 discovery
33 resident
34 visible

Spellography Spelling Inventory — Individual Score Sheet CASE STUDY #4 10/03

Features	Short Vowel	Digraph Trigraph	Blend	VCE	Complex Cons.	Vowel + R	Vowel Teams	Inflections	Syllable Juncture	Prefix	Final Syllable/ Suffix	Root Morph	Extra Point/ Correct	Point Totals
1. shell	e	sh			ll									
2. thing	i	th/ng												
3. cramp	a		cr/mp											
4. slick	i	ck	sl											
5. chunk	u	ch	nk											
6. blotch	o	tch	bl											
7. broke			br	o-e										
8. glade			gl	a-e										
9. fright			fr				igh							
10. quite			qu	i-e										
11. dream			dr				ea							
12. throat			thr				oa							
13. nurse					se	ur								
14. scrape			scr	a-e										
15. charge		ch			-ge	ar								
16. phone		ph		o-e										
17. smudge	u		sm		-dge									
18. point			nt				oi							
19. squirt			squ			ir								
20. drawing			dr				aw	-ing						
21. trapped			tr					-ed	pp					
22. waving								-ing	v (e)					
23. powerful						er	ow				-ful			
24. battle									tt		-tle			
25. refused								-ed		re		fus		
26. lesson									ss		on			
27. pennies								-ies	nn					
28. fraction											-tion	frac		
29. sailor											-or	sail		
30. distance											-ance	dist		
31. conduction										con	-tion	duc		
32. discovery											-ery	cov		
33. resident										re	-ent	sid(e)		
34. visible											-ible	vis		
#/Color Code	7/7	7/8	17/17	5/5	3/4	4/4	6/6	5/5	4/5	3/3	9/10	7/8	[illegible]/34	[illegible]/116

Feature totals in bottom row are colored in as follows: Red = 2+ errors; Yellow = 1 error; Green = 0 errors

11/25/03 CASE STUDY #4

Most Fun Thing At School

The most fun thing at school is orchestra One reason is, you get to learn how to play different kinds of notes. Some of the notes names are open D, E,, F sharp, G, open A, B, C sharp and high D. Another reason is, you have fun. You get to play music with your freinds and listen to beautiful music My final reason is, it is hard work. The instruments are very fragile, and you have to clean the rossin off them Thats the funnest thing at school.

most enjoyable

Case Study #4, Questions for Discussion and Analysis

1. What does this student's *instructional* reading level appear to be?
2. About where does this student rank on the normal curve?
3. Does this student need instruction in decoding skill? What is the basis for your opinion?
4. Does this student need help developing better phonological awareness? What is the basis for your opinion?
5. Would this student benefit from exercises designed specifically to enhance reading fluency? On what do you base your opinion?
6. What is the relationship between fluency and comprehension in this student?
7. Are there other questions you would like to address with additional diagnostic testing, record review, or interviews before planning instruction with this student?
8. What do the writing samples indicate about this student's expressive language and writing abilities?
9. Outline your plan for teaching this student.

   A. Intensity of instruction:

   ____

   ____

   ____

   B. Content emphasis (goals) of instruction:

   ____

   ____

   ____

   C. Possible programs, methods, or approaches:

   ____

   ____

   ____

Case Study #5: Bonnie, Grade 4 (assessed in September)

SKILL ASSESSED	ASSESSMENT TOOL(S)	RESULTS
Silent passage reading with multiple-choice questions, time-limited: **Vocabulary** **Comprehension**	Reading program Placement test	59% correct on silent reading vocabulary, and comprehension at beginning fourth grade-level passage.
Silent word recognition, timed.	(Not given)	
Oral passage reading fluency and accuracy.	Informal reading inventory	66 WCPM, 99% accuracy, on third-grade level. 60% comprehension correct on third-grade passage.
	Gray Oral Reading Test IV (GORT-IV)	50th percentile on accuracy. 2nd percentile on rate. Overall fluency: 9th percentile.
Oral passage reading comprehension.	Gray Oral Reading Test IV (GORT-IV)	16th percentile.
Oral word reading efficiency: **Real words** **Nonsense words**	Test of Word Reading Efficiency (TOWRE)	Real word list: 2.8 grade equivalent. Nonsense word list: 3.2 grade equivalent.
Phonological awareness screen: **Rhyme production** **Syllable counting** **Phoneme segmentation** **Phoneme manipulation and conceptualization**	Informal screening	No errors.
Vocabulary development.	Peabody Picture Vocabulary Test-Third Edition (PPVT-III)	13th percentile (standard score 83).
Inventory of decoding skills: **Areas of strength** **Areas of need**	(Not given)	(Not given)
Developmental spelling inventory: **Number correct** **Areas of need**	(Not given)	(Not given)

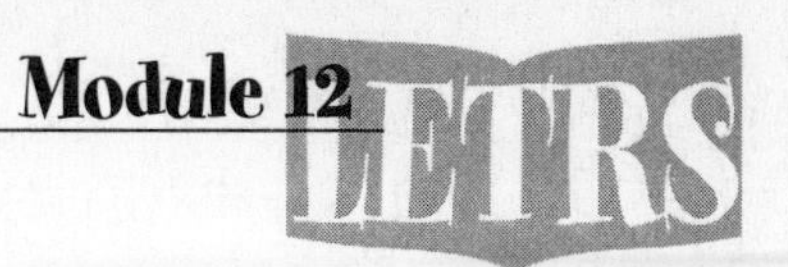

GORT-4

Profile/Examiner Record Booklet
Form A

Gray Oral Reading Tests

Fourth Edition

Section I. Identifying Information

Name CASE STUDY #5 —
Male

School ______ Grade 4
Examiner's Name ______
Examiner's Title ______
Referred by ______
Reason for Referral ______

	Year	Month	Day
Date of Testing	03	8	21
Date of Birth	93	11	15
Test Age	10	7	6

Section II. Record of GORT-4 Scores

Pretest ☐ Posttest ☐

Story #	Rate Score	+	Accuracy Score	=	Fluency Score	Comprehension Score
1	3	+	5	=	8	2
2	4	+	5	=	9	3
3	4	+	5	=	9	2
4	1	+	4	=	5	2
5	1	+	5	=	6	4
6	2	+	5	=	7	2
7	0	+	1	=	1	4
8		+		=		
9		+		=		
10		+		=		
11		+		=		
12		+		=		
13		+		=		
14		+		=		
Total Scores	15		30		45	19
Standard Scores	4		10		6 +	7 = 13
%ile	2		50		9	16
Age Equivalent	7.3		10.3		8.6	8.0
Grade Equivalent	2.2		5.2		3.4	3.0

Sum of Fluency and Comprehension Standard Scores ______
%ile ______
Oral Reading Quotient (ORQ) ______

Section III. Record of Other Test Scores

	Test Name	Date	Test Score	GORT-4 Score Equivalent
1.				
2.				
3.				
4.				

Section IV. Profile of Scores

Standard Score	Rate Score	Accuracy Score	Fluency Score	Comprehension Score	Standard Score	Quotient	Oral Reading Quotient	1. Other ___	2. Other ___	3. Other ___	4. Other ___	Quotient
20	.	.	.	.	20	150	.	.	.	.	.	150
19	.	.	.	.	19	145	.	.	.	.	.	145
18	.	.	.	.	18	140	.	.	.	.	.	140
17	.	.	.	.	17	135	.	.	.	.	.	135
16	.	.	.	.	16	130	.	.	.	.	.	130
15	.	.	.	.	15	125	.	.	.	.	.	125
14	.	.	.	.	14	120	.	.	.	.	.	120
13	.	.	.	.	13	115	.	.	.	.	.	115
12	.	.	.	.	12	110	.	.	.	.	.	110
11	.	.	.	.	11	105	.	.	.	.	.	105
10	—	—	—	—	10	100	—	—	—	—	—	100
9	.	.	.	.	9	95	.	.	.	.	.	95
8	.	.	.	.	8	90	.	.	.	.	.	90
7	.	.	.	.	7	85	.	.	.	.	.	85
6	.	.	.	.	6	80	.	.	.	.	.	80
5	.	.	.	.	5	75	.	.	.	.	.	75
4	.	.	.	.	4	70	.	.	.	.	.	70
3	.	.	.	.	3	65	.	.	.	.	.	65
2	.	.	.	.	2	60	.	.	.	.	.	60
1	.	.	.	.	1	55	.	.	.	.	.	55

4 5 05 04 03

CASE STUDY #5

1-20-03 My favorrate thing this year was. when I heard we won a pizza party for the first time this year. My eyes glinted with joy. I was so. happy we won. When I went home I couldn't stop talking about the pizza party I think I was a little bit to excited. where saposto plain it this friday. Now Im rilly excited now that was the morst excited thing this year.

-15

+19/34

CASE STUDY #5

Spelling Inventory test

1 Shele Shell

2 thing thing

3 Cramp cramP

4 slick slikck

5 Chunk Chunk

6 bloch bloch blotch

7 broke broke

8 glade glade

9 Flite Flite fright

10 quite quite

11 dream dream

12 thrait throat

13 nurse

14 scerape scrape

15 charge

CASE STUDY #5

16 Phome (phone) — Phone 29 (sailor)
17 sinuge (smudge) — 30 (distance)
18 Rount point — 31 condulation
19 Squirt (squirt) — 32 orely
20 draming — 33 (resident)
21 chrapt trapped — 34 visible
22 waving
23 Rowerful — Powerful
24 badle — badle (battle)
25 refuse — refused
26 lesom — leson (lesson)
27 penny — Penny (pennies)
28 fractec — fraction

Spellography Spelling Inventory — Individual Score Sheet

Name CASE STUDY #5 **Date** Sept 03

+19

-15

Features	Short Vowel	Digraph Trigraph	Blend	VCE	Complex Cons.	Vowel + R	Vowel Teams	Inflections	Syllable Juncture	Prefix	Final Syllable/ Suffix	Root Morph	Extra Point/ Correct	Point Totals
(1) shell	e	sh			ll									
(2) thing	i	th/ng												
(3) cramp	a		cr/mp											
(4) slick	i	ck	sl											
(5) chunk	u	ch	nk											
6. blotch ✓	o	tch ✓	bl											
(7) broke			br	o-e										
(8) glade			gl	a-e										
9. fright ✓			fr				igh ✓							
10. quite			qu	i-e										
11. dream			dr				ea							
12. throat			thr				oa							
13. nurse					-se	ur								
14. scrape			scr	a-e										
15. charge		ch			-ge	ar								
16. phone ✓		ph		o-e										
17. smudge ✓	u		sm		-dge ✓									
18. point ✓			nt				oi ✓							
19. squirt ✓			squ			ir ✓								
20. drawing			dr				aw	-ing						
21. trapped			tr ✓					-ed	pp ✓					
22. waving								-ing	-v (e)					
23. powerful						er	ow				-ful			
24. battle ✓									tt ✓		-tle			
25. refused								-ed		re		fus		
26. lesson									ss		-on			
27. pennies ✓								-ies ✓	nn					
28. fraction											-tion	frac		
29. sailor ✓											-or ✓	sail ✓		
30. distance ✓											-ance ✓	dist		
31. conduction										con	-tion	duc		
32. discovery											-ery	cov		
33. resident ✓										re	-ent	sid(e) ✓		
34. visible											-ible	vis		
#/Color Code	7/7	7/8	16/17	5/5	3/4	3/4	4/6	4/5	3/5	3/3	8/10	6/8	/34	/116

Feature totals in bottom row are colored in as follows: Red = 2+ errors; Yellow = 1 error; Green = 0 errors.

Questions for Discussion and Analysis, Case Study #5

1. What does this student's *instructional* reading level appear to be?
2. About where does this student rank on the normal curve? Are there signs of a discrepancy between the student's overall verbal abilities and her reading fluency and comprehension, or is the student functioning at about the expected level?
3. Does this student need instruction in decoding skill? What is the basis for your opinion?
4. Does this student need help developing better phonological awareness? What is the basis for your opinion?
5. Would this student benefit from exercises designed specifically to enhance reading fluency? On what do you base your opinion?
6. Would you expect this student to comprehend well if her fluency and accuracy in word reading were bolstered? What is the implication of your opinion?
7. What other questions would you like to address with additional diagnostic testing, record review, or interviews before planning instruction with this student?
8. Outline your plan for helping this student.

   A. Intensity of instruction:

   ____

   ____

   ____

   B. Content emphasis (goals) of instruction:

   ____

   ____

   ____

   C. Possible programs, methods, or approaches:

   ____

   ____

   ____

Case Study #6: Britney, Grade 5 (assessed in September)

SKILL ASSESSED	ASSESSMENT TOOL(S)	RESULTS
Silent passage reading with multiple-choice questions, time-limited: **Vocabulary** **Comprehension**	Reading program Placement test Unit Test 1	78% total correct. 85% correct on vocabulary. 57% correct on comprehension. 76% correct on comprehension.
Silent word recognition, timed.	(Not given)	
Oral passage reading fluency and accuracy.	Informal reading inventory	111 WCPM, 98% correct, on fifth-grade passage. 60% correct on comprehension questions.
	Gray Oral Reading Test IV (GORT-IV)	(Not given)
Oral passage reading comprehension.	Gray Oral Reading Test IV (GORT-IV)	(Not given)
Oral word reading efficiency: **Real words** **Nonsense words**	Test of Word Reading Efficiency (TOWRE)	(Not given)
Phonological awareness screen: **Rhyme production** **Syllable counting** **Phoneme segmentation** **Phoneme manipulation and conceptualization**	Informal screening	(Not given)
Vocabulary development.	Peabody Picture Vocabulary Test-Third Edition (PPVT-III)	(Not given)
Inventory of decoding skills: **Areas of strength** **Areas of need**	(Oral reading error analysis during passage reading)	**summered/summoned** **inites/ignites** **sniff/snuff** **when/then** **teeny/tiny**
Developmental spelling inventory: **Number correct** **Areas of need**	(Not given)	(Not given)

Unit Test, CASE STUDY #6

Name ______________________ Date ____________

♦ Write a story about the first birthday you can remember. Describe what your day was like and how it felt to be one year older.

THe first birthday I can remember is my 7th birthday. It was on Augest 6, 2003 I Had tons of people there. I had my grandma virg, my grandma bennet, my mom, my dad, Katrina, Quinn, Sami, Stacey Shannon, Justin, and nicole. I had twelve people at my birtday. I went to Fatcity to skate

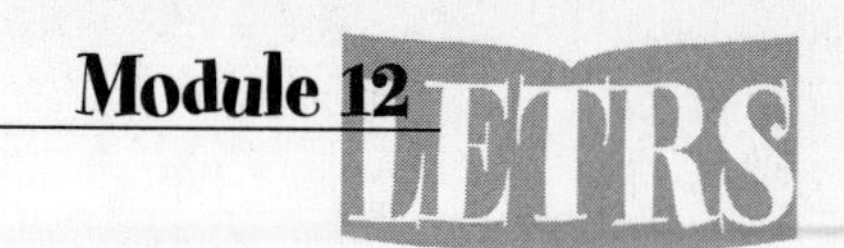

CASE STUDY #6

Spelling test
9-18-03

1. shell
2. thing
3. cramp
4. slick
5. chunk
6. blotch
7. broke
8. glaed ×
9. fright.
10. quite
11. dream
12. throat
13. nurse
14. scrape
15. charge
16. phone
17. smuje ×
18. point
19. squrit ×
20. Drawing
21. traped ×
22. waving
23. powerful
24. battle

Spellography Spelling Inventory — Individual Score Sheet | **Name** CASE STUDY #6 — | **Date** 9/18/03

Features	Short Vowel	Digraph Trigraph	Blend	VCE	Complex Cons.	Vowel + R	Vowel Teams	Inflections	Syllable Juncture	Prefix	Syllable/ Suffix	Root Morph	Extra Point/ Correct	Point Totals
1. shell	e	sh			ll								/	
2. thing	i	th/ng											/	
3. cramp	a		cr/mp										/	
4. slick	i	ck	sl										/	
5. chunk	u	ch	nk										/	
6. blotch	o	tch	bl										/	
7. broke			br	o-e									/	
8. glade			gl	(a-e)										
9. fright			fr				igh						/	
10. quite			qu	i-e									/	
11. dream			dr				ea						/	
12. throat			thr				oa						/	
13. nurse					-se	ur							/	
14. scrape			scr	a-e									/	
15. charge		ch			-ge	ar							/	
16. phone		ph		o-e									/	
17. smudge	u		sm		(-dge)									
18. point			nt				oi						/	
19. squirt			squ			(ir)								
20. drawing			dr				aw	-ing					/	
21. trapped			tr					-ed	(pp)					
22. waving								-ing	-v (e)				/	
23. powerful						er	ow				-ful		/	
24. battle									tt		-tle		/	
25. refused								-ed		re		fus	/	
26. lesson									ss		-on		/	
27. pennies								-ies	nn				/	
28. fraction											-tion	frac	/	
29. sailor											-or	sail	/	
30. distance											-ance	dist	/	
31. conduction										con	-tion	duc	/	
32. discovery											-ery	cov	/	
33. resident										re	-ent	(sid(e))		
34. visible											-ible	vis	/	
#/Color Code	/7	/8	/17	/5	/4	/4	/6	/5	/5	/3	/10	/8	29/34	/116

Feature totals in bottom row are colored in as follows: Red = 2+ errors; Yellow = 1 error; Green = 0 errors.

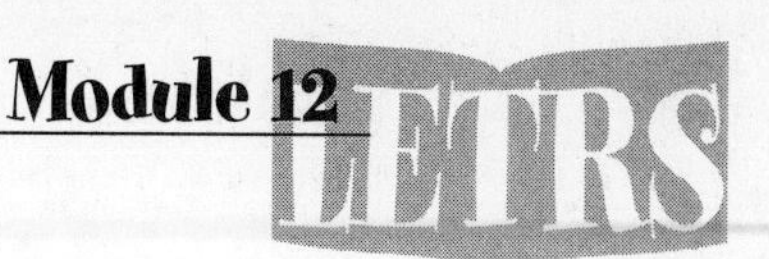

CASE STUDY #6

Chior

PP

11-19-03

writting sample

The most fun activity Ive done this year has been Chior. Monday and Wenesdays we go to choir about 14 people leave for choir there is only 5 people left in our class. I like choir because we get to sing, dance, and play bells. I love to sing, I sing at home all the time in my room. We sing an risers, risers are things that make you taller! We have shirts in Chair they have a silver eagle in the middle of the shirt and on the top it says Eagle chiar there really cool.

Chair is a good activity for people that like to sing and dance. I play C5 on the bells its one of the biggest bells. I lave chair its one of my favarite activitys that I've dome this year. These all are reasons why I like chair so much!

CASE STUDY #5

Grade 5 Informal Reading Inventory

Teacher Page

Passage I

Directions

You are going to read a story about a boy who is trying to start a campfire. Read the story to find out what happens.

Questions

1. C **What was Cody's main problem?** (He was lost in the wilderness.) needed a fire
2. X **Why was he being so careful about starting the fire?** (He had only one match.) didn't want to burn himself
3. C **The story said, ". . . once the match ignites the dry branches, I'll have a fire." What does the word *ignite* mean?** (to light; make something start burning)
4. X **What did Cody do to try to make himself calm?** (Example response: He tried to think peaceful thoughts about pleasant things.) can't remember
5. C **Why did Cody try to find some paper in his bag?** (Example response: Paper would be easier to light than wood or would catch fire more quickly.)

Reading Comprehension	
# Correct	% Score
3/5	60 %

Oral Reading (197 words)	
Accuracy	98 %
Fluency	111 wpm

Scoring Table for Oral Reading	
# Errors	Percent
1–2	99%
3–4 (circled)	98%
5–6	97%
7–8	96%
9–10	95%
11–12	94%
13–14	93%
15–16	92%
17–18	91%
19–20	90%

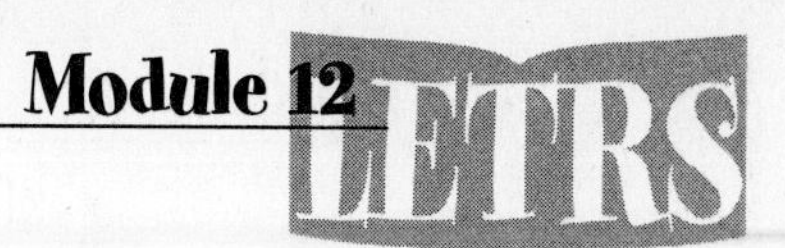

Questions for Discussion and Analysis, Case Study #6

1. What does this student's *instructional* reading level appear to be?

2. About where does this student rank on the normal curve? Are there signs of a discrepancy between the student's overall verbal abilities and her reading fluency and comprehension, or is the student functioning at about the expected level?

3. Does this student need instruction in decoding skill? What is the basis for your opinion?

4. Does this student need help developing better phonological awareness? What is the basis for your opinion?

5. Would this student benefit from exercises designed specifically to enhance reading fluency? On what do you base your opinion?

6. Would you expect this student to comprehend well if her fluency and accuracy in word reading were bolstered? What is the implication of your opinion?

7. What other questions would you like to address with additional diagnostic testing, record review, or interviews before planning instruction with this student?

8. Outline your plan for helping this student.

   A. Intensity of instruction:

   ____

   ____

   ____

   B. Content emphasis (goals) of instruction:

   ____

   ____

   ____

   C. Possible programs, methods, or approaches:

   ____

   ____

   ____

Case Study #7: Corianna, Grade 5 (assessed in September)

SKILL ASSESSED	ASSESSMENT TOOL(S)	RESULTS
Silent passage reading with multiple-choice questions, time-limited: **Vocabulary** **Comprehension**	Reading program Placement test	44% total correct.
Silent word recognition, timed.	(Not given)	
Oral passage reading fluency and accuracy.	Informal reading inventory	45 WCPM, 95% correct, on fifth grade-level passage. 100% correct on comprehension questions.
	Gray Oral Reading Test IV (GORT-IV)	Rate and accuracy (fluency): 1st percentile.
Oral passage reading comprehension.	Gray Oral Reading Test IV (GORT-IV)	37th percentile.
Oral word reading efficiency: **Real words** **Nonsense words**	Test of Word Reading Efficiency (TOWRE)	Real word reading: G.E. 2.4 Nonsense word reading: G.E. 2.2
Phonological awareness screen: **Rhyme production** **Syllable counting** **Phoneme segmentation** **Phoneme manipulation and conceptualization**	Informal screening	Strong on all subskills, no unusual difficulties.
Vocabulary development.	Peabody Picture Vocabulary Test-Third Edition (PPVT-III)	50th percentile.
Inventory of decoding skills: **Areas of strength** **Areas of need**	(Oral reading error analysis during passage reading)	(Not given)
Developmental spelling inventory: **Number correct** **Areas of need**	(Not given)	(Not given)

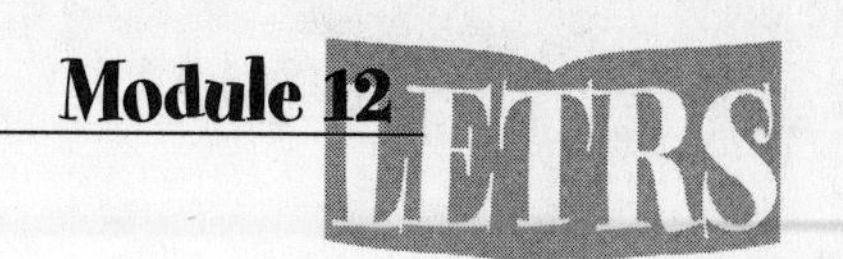

CASE STUDY #7

Grade 5 • IRI

Passage 1

8/19/03

Cody held the last match in his hand and tried to stay calm. He summoned peaceful thoughts of smooth lakes and sweet music until his hand stopped shaking. Everything is going to be all right, Cody told himself. Yes, it's true that I'm lost in the middle of a vast wilderness, but once the match ignites the dry branches, I'll have a fire, and I'll be able to stay warm until someone finds me.

60 secon

As if it could read his mind, the wind picked up. Watch out for me it seemed to whisper as it rustled through the trees, I can snuff out that match you are grasping in your hand.

Carefully placing the match in his pocket, Cody rummaged through his bag for any loose slips of paper. Paper would light quickly, so he could light a dry twig from the flame, and then he could coax the larger pieces of wood in the campfire to catch fire. Unfortunately he did not find any paper, so Cody held his breath as he struck the match. He immediately cupped his hands around the match and held the tiny flame close to the wood, and it caught fire.

CASE STUDY #7

-18 17/35

1. Shell
2. thing
3. cramp
4. Slick
5. Chunk
6. bjoch ✓
7. brack ✓
8. glade
9. fright
10. qaite
11. dream
12. throught ✓
13. herce ✓
14. scap ✓
15. Charge
16. Phone
17. smuse ✓
18. ponte ✓
19. sqart ✓
20. darwing ✓
21. traped ✓
22. wareing ✓
23. powerful
24. battle
25. refused
26. lesson
27. pennyes
28. frachin ✓
29. salon ✓
30. distants ✓
31. conduction
32. discovry ✓
34. resident
35. visuble ✓

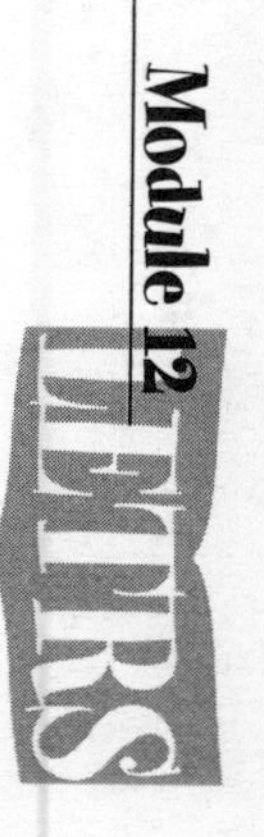

Spellography Spelling Inventory — Individual Score Sheet CASE STUDY #7 6/03

Features	Short Vowel	Digraph Trigraph	Blend	VCE	Complex Cons.	Vowel + R	Vowel Teams	Inflections	Syllable Juncture	Prefix	Final Syllable/ Suffix	Root Morph	Extra Point/ Correct	Point Totals
1. shell	e	sh			ll								1	4
2. thing	i	th/ng											1	4
3. cramp	a		cr/mp										1	4
4. slick	i	ck	sl										1	4
5. chunk	u	ch	nk										1	4
6. blotch	o	tch	bl											2
7. broke			br	o-e										1
8. glade			gl	a-e									1	3
9. fright			fr				igh						1	3
10. quite			qu	i-e									1	3
11. dream			dr				ea						1	3
12. throat			thr				oa							1
13. nurse					-se	ur								0
14. scrape			scr	a-e										1
15. charge		ch			-ge	ar							1	4
16. phone		ph		o-e									1	3
17. smudge	u		sm		-dge									1
18. point			nt				oi							1
19. squirt			squ			ir								1
20. drawing			dr				aw	-ing						1
21. trapped			tr					-ed	pp					2
22. waving								-ing	-v (e)					1
23. powerful						er	ow				-ful		1	4
24. battle									tt		-tle		1	3
25. refused								-ed		re		fus	1	4
26. lesson									ss		-on		1	3
27. pennies								-ies	nn				1	3
28. fraction											-tion	frac		1
29. sailor											-or	sail		1
30. distance											-ance	dist		0
31. conduction										con	-tion	duc	1	4
32. discovery											-ery	cov		1
33. resident										re	-ent	sid(e)	1	4
34. visible											-ible	vis		1
#/Color Code	6/7	7/8	15/17	4/5	2/4	2/4	3/6	5/5	3/5	3/3	6/10	6/8	18/34	80/116

Feature totals in bottom row are colored in as follows: Red = 2+ errors; Yellow = 1 error; Green = 0 errors.

CASE STUDY
#7

Telhether Ball 11/25/03

My favorit thing to do at
school is to play Tethere ball. I
like to play it beacuse it is vally
fun to play. It tells me how
strong I am. I like it because
you get to use your hands
You have to get the ball
around the ball. I like

Unfinished!

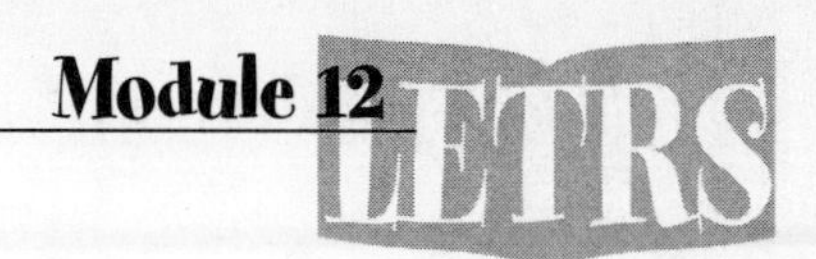

Questions for Discussion and Analysis, Case Study #7

1. What does this student's *instructional* reading level appear to be?
2. About where does this student rank on the normal curve? Are there signs of a discrepancy between the student's overall verbal abilities and her reading fluency and comprehension, or is the student functioning at about the expected level?
3. Does this student need instruction in decoding skill? What is the basis for your opinion?
4. Does this student need help developing better phonological awareness? What is the basis for your opinion?
5. Would this student benefit from exercises designed specifically to enhance reading fluency? On what do you base your opinion?
6. Would you expect this student to comprehend better if her fluency and accuracy in word reading were bolstered? What is the implication of your opinion?
7. What other questions would you like to address with additional diagnostic testing, record review, or interviews before planning instruction with this student?
8. Outline your plan for helping this student:

   A. Intensity of instruction:

   B. Content emphasis (goals) of instruction:

   C. Possible programs, methods, or approaches:

Wrapping Up: Assessment to Guide Instruction

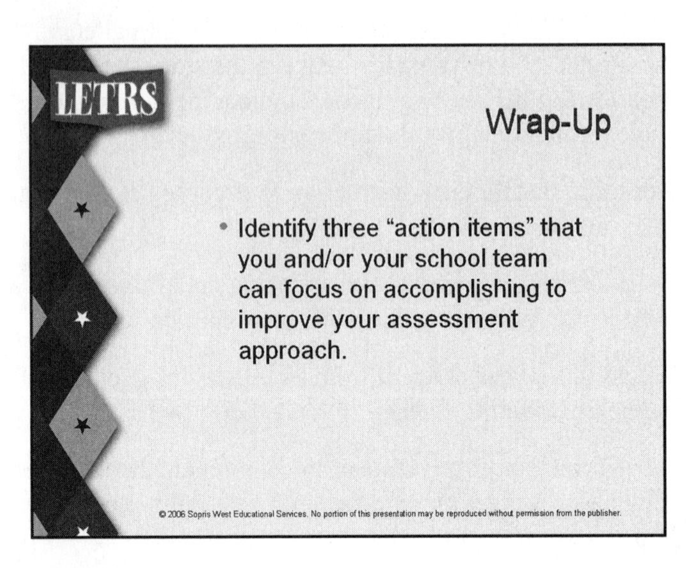

Slide 78

The job of a teacher is to teach as intensively, consistently, and effectively as possible so that most students will learn or progress toward established standards of academic performance. Therefore, assessment should take the minimum amount of time necessary to maximize the effectiveness of instruction. Identifying students in a class who need extra help—and estimating the appropriate focus for that help—are critical exercises. Older students are more challenging than younger ones because more time and effort is needed to successfully remediate reading and writing problems once students have fallen behind (Torgesen, 2004). However, instruction can make a significant difference in long-term academic outcomes, and it is never too late to justify intervention.

Assessment of individuals in a class is done in steps. First, the whole class is screened as efficiently as possible. Second, individual students are selected to receive individual assessments that target the skills most likely to be in need of instruction. Third, the students' strengths and weaknesses in the component skills of reading, spelling, writing, and oral language are assessed. Instructional plans are made and implemented for a specified period of time. Progress monitoring is used to determine if the students are responding to their instructional plan. Changes in program selection, intensity, group composition, or methodology are made if the students are making no progress or—if the student-study team and parent(s) agree—students are referred for additional diagnostic testing.

Oral language and writing skills are difficult areas of performance to quantify, and formal tests for oral language proficiency are less useful to a classroom teacher than direct measures of reading and spelling are likely to be. Rubrics and teacher judgment are important components of any

assessment. Nevertheless, even taking into account all of the inadequacies of current tools, psychological and educational sciences have enhanced our ability to measure, understand, and intervene in reading problems. It behooves us all to make use of those tools and principles that are based on years of scientific investigation. Remember—almost all students can be helped through educational treatments.

Resources for Assessment

Oral Reading Fluency

Analytic Reading Inventory: Prentice-Hall School Division (800-848-9500)

Burns Roe Informal Reading Inventory: Riverside Publishing (800-323-9540)

DIBELS Intermediate: University of Oregon or Sopris West Educational Services (800-547-6747)

Gray Oral Reading Test IV (GORT-IV): Pro-Ed (800-897-3202)

Qualitative Reading Inventory (QRI): Addison Wesley Longman (800-535-4391)

Word Recognition and Spelling

Kaufman Test of Educational Achievement, Spelling Subtest: American Guidance Service (www.ags.com)

All four of these resources are available from Pro-Ed (800-897-3202):

Test of Silent Word Reading Fluency (TOSWRF)

Test of Word Reading Efficiency (TOWRE)

Word Identification and Spelling Test (WIST)

Test of Written Spelling (TWS-4)

Diagnostic Tests

Gallistel-Ellis Test of Coding Skills, Montoge Press, Box 1044, Block Island, RI 02807 (203-488-4294 or 401-466-5975)

Comprehensive Test of Phonological Processing (C-TOPP): Pro-Ed (800-897-3202) or Sopris West Educational Services (800-547-6747)

The CORE Assessing Reading: Multiple Measures Resource Book (www.corelearn.com)

The Decoding Skills Test: Riverside Publishing (800-323-9540)

All three of these resources are available from Pro-Ed (800-897-3202):

Gray Diagnostic Reading Tests (2nd Edition)

Lindamood-Bell Auditory Conceptualization Test (LAC) (3rd Edition)

Rapid Automatic Naming (RAN)

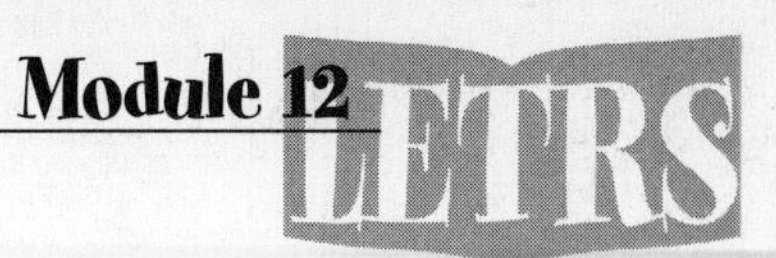

Curriculum-Based Measurements

AIMSweb® (www.AIMSweb.com)

Hosp, M., Howell, K., Hosp, J., & Zucker, S. (in development). *MASI: Multilevel Academic Skills Inventory-Reading.*

Individually Administered Achievement Tests for Classification Purposes

These resources are available from Riverside Publishing (www.riverpub.com):

Woodcock-Johnson® Tests of Achievement (3rd Edition)

Woodcock Reading Mastery Tests

G.R.A.D.E.

References

Adams, M. (1990). *Beginning to read: Thinking and learning about print.* Cambridge, MA: MIT Press.

Apel, K., & Swank, L. K. (1999). Second chances: Improving decoding skills in the older student. *Language, Speech, and Hearing Services in the Schools, 30,* 231–242.

Barr, R., Blachowicz, C. L. Z., Katz, C., & Daufman, B. (2002). *Reading diagnosis for teachers: An instructional approach* (4th ed.). Boston: Allyn & Bacon.

Bear, D., Invernizzi, M., Templeton, S., & Johnston, P. (2003). *Words their way* (3rd ed.). Upper Saddle River, NJ: Prentice Hall.

Catts, H. W., & Kamhi, A. G. (Eds.). (1999). *Language and reading disabilities.* Boston: Allyn & Bacon.

Chard, D. J., Simmons, D. C., & Kame'enui, E. J. (1998). Word recognition: Research bases. In D. C. Simmons & E. J. Kame'enui (Eds.), *What reading research tells us about children with diverse learning needs: Bases and basics* (pp. 239–278). Mahwah, NJ: Lawrence Erlbaum Associates.

Chard, D., Vaughn, S., & Tyler, B. (2002). A synthesis of research on effective interventions for building reading fluency with elementary students with learning disabilities. *Journal of Learning Disabilities, 35,* 386–407.

Deno, S. L., Fuchs, L. S., Marston, D., & Shin, J. (2001). Using curriculum-based measurement to establish growth standards for students with learning disabilities. *School Psychology Review, 22,* 27–48.

Ebbers, S. (2003). *Vocabulary through morphemes: Suffixes, prefixes, and roots for intermediate grades.* Longmont, CO: Sopris West Educational Services.

Ehri, L. (2000). Learning to read and learning to spell: Two sides of a coin. *Topics in Language Disorders, 20*(3), 19–36.

Ehri, L. (2002). Phases of acquisition in learning to read words and implications for teaching. In R. Stainthorp & P. Tomlinson (Eds.), *Learning and teaching reading.* London: British Journal of Educational Psychology Monograph Series II.

Fuchs, L. S., & Fuchs, D. (2003). Can diagnostic reading assessment enhance general educators' instructional differentiation and student learning? In B. R. Foorman (Ed.), *Preventing and remediating reading difficulties: Bringing science to scale* (pp. 325–351). Baltimore: York Press.

Fry, E. (1999). *1000 instant words: The most common words for teaching reading, writing and spelling.* Westminster, CA: Teacher Created Resources.

Good, R. H., III, & Kaminski, R. A. (2002). *Dynamic indicators of basic early literacy skills* (DIBELS™). Longmont, CO: Sopris West Educational Services.

Greene, J. F. (2005). *LANGUAGE!®* (3rd ed.). Longmont, CO: Sopris West Educational Services.

Hasbrouck, J., & Tindal, G. (1992). Curriculum-based oral reading fluency norms for students in grades 2 through 5. *Teaching Exceptional Children, 24*(3), 41–44.

Hasbrouck, J., & Tindal, G. (2005). *Oral reading fluency: 90 years of measurement* (Behavioral Research & Teaching [BRT] Technical Report No. 33). Eugene: University of Oregon, College of Education. Retrieved March 8, 2005, from http://brt.uoregon.edu/techreports/ORF_90Yrs_Intro_TechRpt33.pdf.

Henry, M. (2003). *Unlocking literacy: Effective decoding and spelling instruction.* Baltimore: Paul H. Brookes.

Hirsh, E. D. (2003). Reading comprehension requires knowledge—of words and the world: Scientific insights into the fourth grade slump and the nation's stagnant reading comprehension scores. *American Educator*, *27*(1), 10–22, 28–29, 48.

Hogan, T. P., Catts, H. W., Little, T. D. (in press). The relationship between phonological awareness and reading: Implications for the assessment of phonological awareness. *Language, Speech, and Hearing Services in Schools.*

Hosp, M. K., & Hosp, J. L. (2003). Curriculum-based measurement for reading, spelling, and math: How to do it and why. *Preventing School Failure*, *48*(1), 10–17.

Hosp, M., Howell, K., Hosp, J., & Zucker, S. (in development). *MASI: Multilevel academic skills inventory-Reading.*

Learning First Alliance. (2000). *Every child reading: A professional development guide.* Washington, DC: Author.

Masterson, J., & Apel, K. (2000). Spelling assessment: Charting a path to optimal intervention. *Topics in Language Disorders*, *20*(3), 50–66.

Masterson, J. J., Apel, K., & Wasowicz, J. *SPELL Examiner's Manual: Spelling performance evaluation for language and literacy.* Evanston, IL: Learning by Design. (www.learningbydesign.com)

Mather, N., Hammill, D. D., Allen, E. A., & Roberts, R. (2004). *Test of Silent Word Reading Fluency.* Austin, TX: Pro-Ed.

Mercer, C. D., Campbell, K. U., Miller, M. D., Mercer, K. D., & Lane, H. B. (2000). Effects of a reading fluency intervention for middle-schoolers with specific learning disabilities. *Learning Disabilities Research and Practice*, *15*(4), 179–189.

Moats, L. C. (1996). Phonological spelling errors in the writing of dyslexic adolescents. *Reading and Writing: An Interdisciplinary Journal*, *8*, 105–119.

Moats, L. C. (1999, June). *Teaching reading* is *rocket science* (Item No. 39-0372). Washington, DC: American Federation of Teachers.

Moats, L. C. (2001). When older kids can't read. *Educational Leadership*, *58*(6), 36–40.

Moats, L. C., & Rosow, B. (2002). *Spellography: A student road map to better spelling.* Longmont, CO: Sopris West Educational Services.

National Center for Education Statistics (NCES). (2003). *National Assessment of Educational Progress (NAEP) 2003 State Snapshot Reports.* Washington, DC: NCES, Institute for Education Sciences, United States Department of Education.

Rayner, K., Foorman, B. F., Perfetti, C. A., Pesetsky, D., & Seidenberg, M. S. (2001). How psychological science informs the teaching of reading. *Psychological Science in the Public Interest*, *2*(2), 31–74.

Shaywitz, S. (2003). *Overcoming dyslexia: A new and complete science-based program for reading problems at any level.* New York: Alfred Knopf.

Torgesen, J. T. (2004). Avoiding the devastating downward spiral: The evidence that early intervention prevents reading failure. *American Educator*, *28*(3), 6–9, 12–13, 17–19, 45.

Torgesen, J. K., Rashotte, C. A., Alexander, A., Alexander, J., & MacPhee, K. (2003). Progress toward understanding the instructional conditions necessary for remediating reading difficulties in older children. In B. R. Foorman (Ed.), *Preventing and remediating reading difficulties: Bringing science to scale* (pp. 275–297). Baltimore: York Press.

Torgesen, J. K., Wagner, R., & Rashotte, C. (1999). *Test of word reading efficiency* (TOWRE). Austin, TX: Pro-Ed.

Vaughn, S., & Linan-Thompson, S. (2003). Group size and time allotted to intervention: Effects for students with reading difficulties. In B. Foorman (Ed.), *Preventing and remediating reading difficulties: Bringing science to scale* (pp. 299–324). Baltimore: York Press.

Wolf, M., O'Brien, B., Adams, K. D., Joffe, T., Jeffrey, J., Lovett, M., et al. (2003). Working for time: Reflections on naming speed, reading fluency, and intervention. In B. R. Foorman (Ed.), *Preventing and remediating reading difficulties: Bringing science to scale* (pp. 355–379). Baltimore: York Press.

Internet Links **(All links retrieved March 10, 2005)**

The Adult Reading Components Study—National Institute for Literacy (NIFL) (www.nifl.gov/readingprofiles)

American Speech-Language-Hearing Association. (2001). *Roles and responsibilities of speech-language pathologists with respect to reading and writing in children and adolescents* (Position statement). ASHA Supplement 21, 17–28. Rockville, MD: Author.

BIG IDEAS in Beginning Reading (http://reading.uoregon.edu)

National Reading Panel Report (http://www.nichd.nih.gov/publications/pubskey.cfm?from=nrp)

Reading Rockets, WETA, Washington, DC (www.readingrockets.com)

LETRS
Language Essentials for Teachers of Reading and Spelling

Glossary

affix: a morpheme or meaningful part of a word attached before or after a root to modify its meaning; a category that subsumes prefixes, suffixes, and infixes

alphabetic principle: the principle that letters are used to represent individual phonemes in the spoken word; a critical insight for beginning reading and spelling

alphabetic writing system: a system of symbols that represent each consonant and vowel sound in a language

Anglo-Saxon: Old English; a Germanic language spoken in Britain before the invasion of the Norman French in 1066

base word: a free morpheme to which affixes can be added, usually of Anglo-Saxon origin

closed syllable: a written syllable containing a single vowel letter that ends in one or more consonants. The vowel sound is short.

concept: an idea that links other facts, words, and ideas together into a coherent whole

conjunction: a word that connects a dependent clause to a dependent clause, or a word that connects two independent clauses

consonant: a phoneme (speech sound) that is not a vowel, and that is formed with obstruction of the flow of air with the teeth, lips, or tongue; also called a *closed sound* in some instructional programs. English has 40 or more consonants.

consonant blend: two or three adjacent consonants before or after the vowel in a syllable (e.g., **st-**, **spr-**, **-lk**, **-mp**)

consonant digraph: a letter combination that represents one speech sound that is not represented by either letter alone (e.g., **sh**, **th**, **wh**, **ph**, **ch**, **ng**)

Consonant -le syllable: a written syllable found at the ends of words such as *paddle*, *single*, and *rubble*

cumulative instruction: teaching that proceeds in additive steps, building on what was previously taught

decodable text: text in which a high proportion of words (80%–90%) comprise sound-symbol relationships that have already been taught; used for the purpose of providing practice with specific decoding skills; a bridge between learning phonics and the application of phonics in independent reading of text

decoding: the ability to translate a word from print to speech, usually by employing knowledge of sound-symbol correspondences; also the act of deciphering a new word by sounding it out

diagnostic assessment: after screening, the use of additional measures to determine more precisely the nature of a student's difficulties and/or the specific skills that need to be taught

dialects: mutually intelligible versions of the same language with systematic differences in phonology, word use, and/or grammatical rules

DIBELS: Dynamic Indicators of Basic Early Literacy Skills (a literacy assessment series by Roland H. Good III and Ruth A. Kaminski, University of Oregon)

dictation: the teacher repeats words, phrases, or sentences slowly while students practice writing them accurately

digraph: (*see* **consonant digraph**)

diphthong: a vowel produced by the tongue shifting position during articulation; a vowel that feels as if it has two parts, especially the vowels spelled **ou** and **oi**. Some linguistics texts also classify all tense (long) vowels as diphthongs

direct instruction: the teacher defines and teaches a concept, guides students through its application, and arranges for extended guided practice until mastery is achieved

dyslexia: an impairment of reading accuracy and fluency attributable to an underlying phonological processing problem, usually associated with other kinds of language processing difficulties

efficient assessment: an assessment that takes a minimum amount of time, costs a minimum amount of money, and provides valid, reliable information about a student's future academic outcomes or present levels of performance

generalization: a pattern in the spelling system that generalizes to a substantial family of words

grapheme: a letter or letter combination that spells a phoneme; can be one, two, three, or four letters in English (e.g., **e**, **ei**, **igh**, **eigh**)

high-frequency word: a word that occurs very often in written text; a word that is among the 300 to 500 most often used words in English text

inflection: a type of bound morpheme; a grammatical ending that does not change the part of speech of a word but that marks its tense, number, or degree in English (e.g., **-ed**, **-s**, **-ing**)

integrated: when lesson components are interwoven and flow smoothly together

irregular word: a word that does not follow common phonic patterns; a word that is not a member of word family (e.g., *were*, *was*, *laugh*, *been*)

meaning processor: the neural networks that attach meanings to words that have been heard or decoded

morpheme: the smallest meaningful unit of the language

morphology: the study of the meaningful units in the language and how they are combined in word formation

multisyllabic: having more than one syllable

narrative text: text that tells about sequences of events, usually with the structure of a story (fiction or nonfiction); often contrasted with *expository text*, which reports factual information and relationships among ideas

nonsense word: a word that sounds like a real English word and can be sounded out, but that has no assigned meaning (e.g., *lemidation*)

normal curve equivalent: a statistic that reflects a band of the normal curve in which a given test score lies; a commonly used measure of relative standing

onset-rime: the natural division of a syllable into two parts, the onset coming before the vowel and the rime including the vowel and the letters that follow it (e.g., *pl-an*, *shr-ill*)

orthographic processor: the neural networks responsible for perceiving, storing, and retrieving the letter sequences in words

orthography: a writing system for representing language

outcome assessment: an academic achievement test (usually end-of-year) that allows a student's performance to be compared to a national or regional standard for age and/or grade level

percentile: a measure of relative standing that reflects an individual student's performance in a rank-order scale of 1 to 99; thus, the 40th percentile is better than that of 40 students out of 100, and worse than 59 students out of 100

phoneme: a speech sound that combines with others in a language system to make words

phoneme awareness (*also* **phonemic awareness**): the conscious awareness that words are made up of segments of our own speech that are represented with letters in an alphabetic orthography

phoneme-grapheme mapping: an activity for showing how letters and letter combinations correspond to the individual speech sounds in a word

phonics: the study of the relationships between letters and the sounds they represent; also used as a descriptor for code-based instruction in reading (e.g., "the phonics approach" or "phonic reading")

phonological awareness: metalinguistic awareness of all levels of the speech-sound system, including word boundaries, stress patterns, syllables, onset-rime units, and phonemes; a more encompassing term than *phoneme awareness*

phonological processor: a neural network in the frontal and temporal areas of the brain, usually the left cerebral hemisphere, that is specialized for speech-sound perception and memory

phonology: the rule system within a language by which phonemes can be sequenced and uttered to make words

pragmatics: the system of rules and conventions for using language and related gestures in a social context

predictor: a measure of present performance that has been validated or shown to predict future achievement levels in a given academic area, such as reading

prefix: a morpheme that precedes a root and that contributes to or modifies the meaning of a word; a common linguistic unit in Latin-based words

progress monitoring: frequent assessment of academic growth toward an established goal to measure response to instruction; usually accomplished with brief, specific measures of relevant academic skills, such as oral reading fluency and accuracy

reading fluency: the speed of oral reading, measured by words correct per minute (WCPM); the ability to read text with sufficient speed to support comprehension

reliable: likely to yield the same score if the test could be given on consecutive days or at the same time by different examiners

risk indicator: a task that predicts an outcome on high-stakes reading tests

root: a bound morpheme, usually of Latin origin, that cannot stand alone but that is used to form a family of words with related meanings

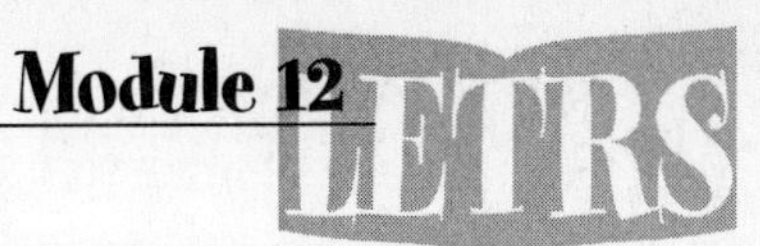

schwa: the "empty" vowel in an unaccented syllable (e.g., the last syllables of *circus* and *bagel*)

screening: a brief, economical assessment that allows a rough but reliable sorting of students into those at risk for problems and those not at risk

semantics: the study of word and phrase meanings

silent-letter spelling: a consonant grapheme with a silent letter and a letter that corresponds to the vocalized sound (e.g., **kn**, **wr**, **gn**)

sound blending: saying the individual phonemes in a word, then putting the sounds together to make a whole word

sound-symbol correspondence: same as *phoneme-grapheme correspondence*; the rules and patterns by which letters and letter combinations represent speech sounds

speed drills: one-minute timed exercises to build fluency in learned skills

standard score: a measure of relative standing, often based on a scale with a mean of 100 and a standard deviation of 15; unlike percentiles or other rank-order systems, standard scores represent equal intervals on a continuum

stop: a type of consonant that is spoken with one push of breath and not continued or carried out, including / p /, / b /, / t /, / d /, / k /, / g /

structural analysis: the study of affixes, base words, and roots

suffix: a derivational morpheme added to the end of a root or base word that often changes the word's part of speech and modifies its meaning

summative assessment: an end-of-year assessment, usually with a comprehensive achievement test, that evaluates overall student progress during the school year

syllabic consonants: / m /, / n /, / l /, / r / can do the job of a vowel and make an unaccented syllable at the ends of words such as *rhythm*, *mitten*, *little*, and *letter*

syllable: the unit of pronunciation that is organized around a vowel; it may or may not have consonants before or after the vowel

text generator: the part of the brain that translates ideas into words as we are writing

transcription: the act of putting words down in writing or typing; the act of producing written words by hand once the brain has generated them

valid: a measure that assesses what it purports to measure; established by showing what the measure is related to and by justifying its structure and contents on accepted theoretical grounds

vowel: one of a set of 15 vowel phonemes in English, not including vowel-**r** combinations; an open phoneme that is the nucleus of every syllable; classified by tongue position and height (high-low, front-back)

whole language: a philosophy of reading instruction that emphasizes the importance of learning to recognize words as whole entities through encounters in meaningful contexts rather than focusing on phonics and phonology

word family: a group of words that share a rime (a vowel plus the consonants that follow; e.g., **-ame**, **-ick**, **-out**)

word recognition: the ability to identify the spoken word that a printed word represents; to name the word on the printed page

writing process approach: instruction in written expression that emphasizes a progression through three major phases, including: (a) planning and organizing the piece; (b) writing a draft; and (c) getting feedback and revising for publication

Appendix A

Answer Key to Exercises #4 and #5

Exercise #4: Spelling Inventory

Spelling Inventory // Set B – Individual Score Sheet Name: Ben Date_______

FEATURES	Short vowel	Digrph Trigrph	Blend	VCE	Complex Cons.	Vowel + R	Vowel Teams	Inflec-tions	Syllable juncture	Prefix	Final Syllable / suffix	Root morph	Extra Point/ correct	Point Totals
1. theft	e	th	ft											
2. still	i		st		ll									
3. trunk	u		tr/nk											
4. clock	o	-ck	cl											
5. string	i	-ng	str											
6. sketch	e	-tch	sk											
7. choke		ch		o-e										
8. grade			gr	a-e										
9. slight			sl				igh							
10. quake			qu	a-e										
11. sneak			sn				ea							
12. coach		-ch					oa							
13. burnt			nt			ur								
14. splice			spl	i-e										
15. barge					-ge	ar								
16. quote			qu	o-e										
17. sludge	u		sl		-dge									
18. moist			-st				oi							
19. swirl			sw			ir								
20. yawning							aw	-ing						
21. dragged			dr					-ed	gg					
22. tracing			tr					-ing	a-(e)					
23. showered		sh				er	ow	-ed						
24. quitting								-ing	tt					
25. expressed								-ed		ex		press		
26. sudden									dd		-en			
27. bunnies								-ies	nn					
28. traction											-tion	trac		
29. instructor										in	-or	struct		
30. attendance										at	-ance	tend		
31. confession										con	-sion	fes(s)		
32. reportable						or				re	-able	port		
33. difference										dif	-ence	fer		
34. flexible											-ible	flex		
#/Color Code	5 /7	6 /7	17/19	4 /5	2 /3	1 /5	1 /6	3 /7	0 /5	0 /6	0 /8	0 /8	10 /34	/120

Feature totals in bottom row are colored in as follows: Red= 2+ errors; Yellow = 1 error; Green = 0 errors

2

Exercise #5: Spelling Errors for Analysis

- Below are spelling errors typical of three students.

1. Which student is phonologically challenged?

   Student 2: (a) confuses voiceless /p/ with voiced /b/ in **sbek** and voiced /j/ with voiceless /ch/ in **jarj**; (b) omits consonant sounds in blends (**sich**, **sap**, **suj**, **pt**, **st**); and (c) cannot spell phonetically. This student is an early alphabetic speller.

2. Which student is generally aware of the sounds but uses the wrong letters for those sounds and does not know rules for adding endings?

   Student 1 can spell phonetically; most of the sounds are represented. However, this student does not know: (a) the conventional graphemes for final /k/ after a short vowel (**-ck**) or /ch/ after a short vowel (**-tch**); (b) the right letters for the **scr-** blend; (c) **squ** as a spelling for /skw/; or (d) the **tr-** blend in the word **trapped**. This student also does not drop the silent **-e** in the word **waving** or double the letter **p** in the word **trapped**.

3. Which student is quite solid on one-syllable words but insecure with written syllable patterns, endings, and word structure (compounds, base words and endings, prefixes, suffixes, roots)?

   Student 3 is the most accurate speller but does not yet know: (a) when to apply the Doubling Rule; (b) when to double a final consonant before an **-ed** ending; (c) how to spell the **-ful** suffix; or (d) when the Consonant-**le** pattern is used.

Words Given	Student #1	Student #2	Student #3
speck	spek	sbek	speck
switch	swich	sich	switch
throat	throte	trot	throat
nurse	nurs	nrs	nurse
scrape	skrape	sap	scrape
charge	chardge	jarj	charge
phone	fone	fon	phone
smudge	smuge	suj	smuge
point	poit	pt	point
squirt	skwirt	st	squirt
drawing	droughing	gwiig	drawwing
trapped	chrapt		trapted
waving	waiveing		waveing
powerful	pourfull		powerfull
battle	badl		battel
fever	fevr		feaver
lesson	lesin		
pennies	penees		
fraction	frakshun		
sailor	saler		

Appendix B

Beginning Decoding Skills Survey

Beginning Decoding Skills Survey (Linda Farrell)

General Instructions

Record scores and errors on the Scoring Form. If the student makes an error, *be sure to record what the student reads*. If the student doesn't get the correct answer, record the number of times it takes to get the answer correct.

Directions:

1. Give the student the "Words and Sentences to Read" page.
2. Ask the student to read the words at the top of the page. The student can select whether to read across or down. Stop when the student misses three in a row and ask the student if he or she can read any other words in that part of the page.
3. Ask the student to read the sentences in the middle of the page.
4. Ask the student to read the nonsense words at the bottom of the page. You may have to explain that nonsense words can be read, but they don't mean anything.
5. Record error patterns on the Error Pattern Chart.
    - Attach the Beginning Decoding Skills Survey Scoring Form to the Error Pattern Chart.
    - Write the specific error the student made next to the word on the Error Pattern Chart.
    - Put a check in the box in the chart that describes student errors.

Using the Error Pattern Chart:

Teach the skills the student is missing, which will be indicated by more than one checkmark in a column with the missing skill, or area of weakness, as the header. In general, begin teaching the skill that is checked and farthest to the left on the chart.

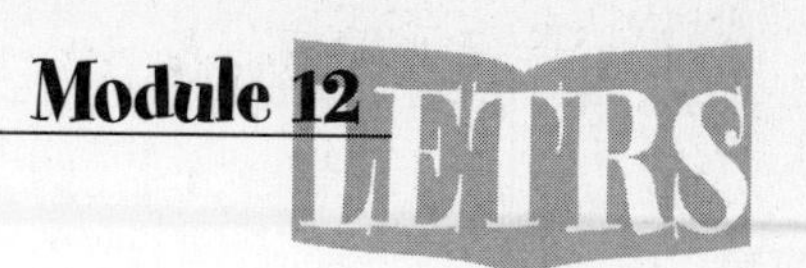

Beginning Decoding Skills Survey

Scoring Form

Student Name ______________________________ Grade __________

Date of assessment ______________________________

Assessment Administrator ______________________________

CODING
✓ = Read correctly
2x or **3x** = Read correctly second or third time
DK = Don't know
NT = Not tried or skipped

Write mispronunciations, substitutions, or incorrectly read words next to or above word.

Real Words

High Frequency Words	*CVC Words*	*Digraphs*	*Blends*
see ________	rag ________	rich ________	dust ________
one ________	lid ________	shop ________	step ________
play ________	dot ________	tack ________	trip ________
you ________	hum ________	whip ________	pond ________
are ________	bet ________	thin ________	brag ________

Sentences

1. The cat hid in a box.
2. The fish is still in the deep lake.
3. Seven pink shellfish were in my bathtub.

Nonsense Words

CVC	*Digraphs*
vop ______________	shap ____________
yuz ______________	thit______________
zin _______________	chut______________
keb ______________	wheck ____________

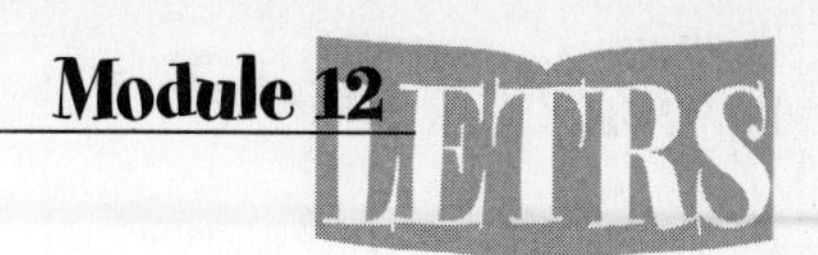

Words and Sentences to Read

see	rag	rich	dust
one	lid	shop	step
play	dot	tack	trip
you	hum	whip	pond
are	bet	thin	drag

---

1. The cat hid in a box.
2. The fish is still in the deep lake.
3. Seven pink shellfish were in my bathtub.

---

vop	shap
yuz	thit
zin	chut
keb	wheck

Beginning Decoding Skills Survey

Error Pattern Chart

Attach the Beginning Decoding Skills Survey Scoring Form.

Cross off all words not attempted and put a check in the "No Try" box.

Write the words read incorrectly on the line next to the word attempted.

Put a check in the box in the chart that describes the error(s) for each word.

Observations: (check all that apply)

- ❑ Slow
- ❑ Quick to guess
- ❑ Guesses after trying to decode using letter-sound analysis
- ❑ Reads sound-by-sound, but cannot blend
- ❑ Possible b/d reversal

Comments (*continue on back*):

REAL WORDS		Error Patterns: No Try	Sight Word	Consonants: Initial	Consonants: Final	Short Vowels	Extra Sound(s) Added	Digraphs	Blends	Long Vowels	Syllables
High Frequency Words											
1	see										
2	one										
3	play										
4	you										
5	are										
CVC Words											
6	rag										
7	lid										
8	dot										
9	hum										
10	bet										
Digraphs and Short Vowels											
11	rich										
12	shop										
13	tack										
14	whip										
15	thin										
Blends and Short Vowels											
16	dust										
17	step										
18	trip										
19	pond										
20	brag										
SENTENCES											
1	The cat hid in a box.										
2	The fish is still in the deep lake.										
3	Seven pink shellfish were in my bathtub.										
NONSENSE WORDS											
CVC											
21	vop										
22	yuz										
23	zin										
24	keb										
Digraphs											
25	shap										
26	thit										
27	chut										
28	wheck